SCHOLASTIC

Read-Aloud Plays:
Classic Short Stories

Original Play Adaptations by Mack Lewis

NEW YORK • TORONTO • LONDON • AUCKLAND • SYDNEY
MEXICO CITY • NEW DELHI • HONG KONG • BUENOS AIRES

Teaching Resources

To Lauren T.

Editor: Maria L. Chang
Cover design by Maria Lilja
Interior design by Kathy Massaro
Illustrations by Dani Jones

ISBN: 978-0-545-20456-9

Printed in the U.S.A.

6 7 8 9 10 40 20 19 18 17 16 15 14

Contents

Introduction 4

The Legend of Sleepy Hollow
by Washington Irving ✠ (United States, 1820) 7

The Nose
by Nikolai Gogol ✠ (Russia, 1836) 14

The Tell-Tale Heart
by Edgar Allan Poe ✠ (United States, 1843) 23

A Christmas Carol
by Charles Dickens ✠ (England, 1843) 30

The Necklace
by Guy de Maupassant ✠ (France, 1884) 38

Rikki-Tikki-Tavi
by Rudyard Kipling ✠ (England, 1894) 46

The Gift of the Magi
by O. Henry ✠ (United States, 1906) 55

The Open Window
by Saki (H. H. Munro) ✠ (England, 1914) 62

Literary Elements/Story Discussion reproducible 68

Play Performance Scoring Guide 69

Discussion Questions Answer Key 70

Introduction

Given competition from texting, iPods, Wii, and YouTube, it's harder than ever to get young people excited about reading—especially classic literature. But *Read-Aloud Plays: Classic Short Stories* will not only engage your students in the likes of Poe, Irving, Kipling, and others, it will also build their fluency and comprehension skills.

Each of the plays is based upon works society has deemed worth knowing. The fact that these stories are one to two centuries old yet remain readily recognizable proves their staying power. But each of these plays has also been kid-tested. In fact, several have appeared in Scholastic's popular classroom language arts magazine *Storyworks*, receiving rave reviews from teachers and students alike.

The age of these stories also puts them in the public domain. While *these plays* are original adaptations and therefore copyrighted, the original stories no longer are. You can download printable versions, along with a wide variety of support material, at *mackowiecki.com*. Depending on your grade level and the difficulty of the original text, you may want to consider having your students read the original story while working on the corresponding adapted play.

Included at the beginning of each play is a list of ten vocabulary words or phrases. Make sure students are familiar with the pronunciation and meaning of these words prior to reading the script independently. We haven't provided definitions here, allowing you to teach the vocabulary using the methodology of your choice.

We've also included a set of questions within each play. The questions are designed to stimulate discussion as you read the play together, but they're also suitable for homework responses or short-answer quizzes. You may want students to complete a full reading before considering the questions, and we encourage you to review the answer key (pages 70–72) prior to discussion. No doubt you'll develop your own questioning strategies, and you and your students will likely see some recurring themes common to these literature periods.

There are several enjoyable and effective ways to produce plays in your classroom—Readers Theater, simple performance, radio drama, puppet shows, and full-blown stage productions, to name a few. Whichever format you choose, the most important factor is that students read the same script repetitively. Divide your class into groups based on the number of parts in each play you plan to use. I try to use three groups of 8 to 12 students. The size of your class and the number of characters in each play will dictate whether any of your students will need to double up and perform more than one role.

Once you have your "play groups," you'll need to rotate them through a station in which they meet with you. Other students can do seatwork, read independently, or meet with parent-volunteers for guided reading activities while they wait for their turn at the director's table. I spend about 20 minutes with each group "practicing" the given play, meeting two or three times a week. After a week or so, we begin rehearsing. After another week or two, we're ready to perform. Allot about three weeks to work on a play. After a month, students begin losing interest. Aim for four weeks, but be flexible.

When in the group, I require my students to follow along so they know when to read their lines. It's also beneficial for their eyes to see words their ears are hearing others read. This way, even struggling students with only a few spoken lines get just as much practice as the "stars." I also ask them to let me do the correcting and cueing so that we are sensitive to the emotional and instructional needs of each individual student.

Building Fluency With Play Scripts

Many kids begin school already knowing how to read. They haven't had formal lessons. Their parents haven't been trained in the latest methodology. They haven't used a single worksheet or textbook. Yet here they are reading. Why?

Consider for a moment how your own children learned to read. If they're like most kids, they had a few favorites among their ready supply of books. I recall my oldest boy latching on to *Amos & Boris* and a Sesame Street book entitled *Don't Forget the Oatmeal!* As a toddler, he would ask us to read these books over and over again. Soon, he started reading them to us. "He's not really reading," we told ourselves. "He's heard the book so many times, he's just memorized the words."

But based on brain research by psychologist Lev Vygotsky and others, some experts believe the difference between reading and memorization is slight. Kids get an emotional charge out of reading proficiently—whether memorized or not. The positive charge actually produces chemicals that form the neural pathways that make reading (and learning) possible. Because our son had consumed *Don't Forget the Oatmeal!* so frequently, he had mastered the text, prompting his brain to construct new pathways.

Now, consider what we often do in the classroom. We take a book, article, or story and ask kids to read it one time. We expect mastery on their first attempt. We ask kids to pass computerized tests, complete worksheets, and discuss content after just a single reading. We've assumed that language is language, that if they can decode they should be able to read anything at their grade level. It's a fallacy and a tragedy. Instead of experiencing a positive emotion that builds pathways, many kids in this situation suffer a negative emotion that causes them to withdraw and resist reading altogether. Don't assume it's just your lower-performing students either. Watch carefully when you ask students to read aloud in class; many of your brightest kids who seem to be good readers are just as reluctant as your poor readers. It's not simply that they're shy; they don't want to risk experiencing the negative emotions they feel when they stumble over, mispronounce, or don't understand a word.

Asking a young reader to read aloud a piece of text he or she is looking at for the very first time is akin to asking a musician to perform publicly a piece of music he or she has never seen before. Only the most talented can do it, and even they rarely do. Just as music is a language that requires repetition for mastery, so too is reading. Your students need opportunities to "sight-read," to practice, and then to "perform" the material you want them to master. Plays are the perfect format.

Because we've trained kids that a book is something to be read only once, few third graders are willing to give *James and the Giant Peach* a second go-round. Few second graders will read *Stellaluna* more than once or twice. Give children a script and schedule a public performance, however, and they'll be more than happy to read and reread it 20 to 30 times! By the time they're asked to read the script in front of the class, even your struggling readers will be able to read fluently. Even your "shy" kids will be willing to read out loud.

Read-Aloud Plays: Classic Short Stories gives you the opportunity to teach repetitive reading without the resistance you would get asking a child to reread a traditional text. Students acquire mastery, which chemically changes the brain, making them more fluent readers who are better able to comprehend.

Assessment and Post-Performance Discussion

It's the emotional charge that releases the brain-changing chemicals, therefore it is important that assessment be handled delicately. You want your students—even your poorest readers—to step off the stage feeling like a master of the English language, so the conclusion of the performance isn't the time to be dishing out Cs and Ds in reading. If you've done a good job running your practice sessions, every student should be earning high marks. Consider using a rubric or scoring guide identifying standards for a successful performance (see page 69). The rubric might include fluency, volume, positioning, characterization, and more. Discuss these standards before you begin rehearsals, then consistently revisit these factors as you practice.

Upon conclusion of a given play, have your actors remain before the class. Ask the class: *What did they do well?* The audience will provide feedback. "Maureen spoke loudly" is one comment you're likely to hear. "Othar said his lines just like he talks" and "Toni put character in her voice" are others. Not only does the audience provide valuable feedback for the performers, they're actually synthesizing evaluative factors they will then apply to their own performance. You can also ask, "What do they need to work on?" and you'll get answers such as "Matt needed to keep from turning his back to the audience," "Paulie lost her spot; she needed to follow along better," and "Trey needs to keep his script away from his face so the audience can hear him." You'll find that because these comments come from other students rather than the teacher, the performers are better able to receive them without the negative emotional charge a grade has. Note also that this is how adults evaluate theater performances in real life; we just don't get to share our opinions with the actors. When using this approach over a number of plays, your students will learn to assess themselves, becoming adept performers and solid readers.

Evaluating the play and/or story itself for its entertainment value and academic content may also be important. You can ask your students the same questions you might ask in any literary or social studies discussion: *What did this play teach you? Did you enjoy the story? What is the setting? Was this story realistic or unrealistic? What does the author want you to believe about life in India?* Whatever is called for by your particular language arts or social studies standards, you can address it through a play. We've included a short-answer assessment activity covering basic literary elements on page 68. It can be used with any work of fiction.

Of course, there are many ways to utilize play scripts in the classroom, and there's certainly nothing wrong with using a script purely for the pleasure of reading. Whether read just once or 20 times over, I hope your students find *Read-Aloud Plays: Classic Short Stories* a real kick in the pants.

THE LEGEND OF Sleepy Hollow

by Washington Irving (United States, 1820)

The Headless Horseman conjures up images of ghosts and zombies—always engaging topics for young students. But "Sleepy Hollow" is more than just a ghost story. Set during the post–Revolutionary War period, it's the story of schoolmaster Ichabod Crane, one of the most interesting characters in American literature. Students will enjoy theorizing about the truth behind the Horseman. Did Irving intend for readers to believe the legend? Or are there other explanations for Ichabod's disappearance? This play harkens back to the days of Old English and the Jolly Roger, so encourage your kids to try out their best pirate accent!

Diedrich Knickerbocker: Our storyteller

Stage Director: Directs the action in the play

Old Woman 1

Old Woman 2

Ichabod Crane: The superstitious schoolmaster

Katrina Van Tassel: The village beauty

Brom Bones: The village brute

Baltus Van Tassel: Katrina's father

Van Ax: Villager/party guest

Van Ripper: Villager/party guest

Vanderblood: Villager/party guest

Brouwer: Villager/party guest

Nonspeaking parts:

Gunpowder: Ichabod's horse

The Headless Horseman: Silent, but dreadful

Vocabulary

entranced, brooding, tethered, hymn, pommel, mischief, shriek, decrepit, misshapen, flimsy

Scene 1: Sleepy Hollow

KNICKERBOCKER: I was never one for ghost stories, not till I happened upon a little village called Sleepy Hollow. Had I not seen it for myself, I would have dismissed it as a bit of superstition, but this . . . I shudder to think of it!

STAGE DIRECTOR: A lanky fellow enters, entranced by a book. As he walks, he absentmindedly whistles "Yankee Doodle."

KNICKERBOCKER: My name is Diedrich Knickerbocker. The year was 1790, and as I wandered the drowsy shadows of the Hollow, I encountered a man named Ichabod Crane.

> **Think About It**
> The setting of a story is its time (or era) and place. How would you describe the setting of this story?

OLD WOMAN 1: Look here. It's the new schoolmaster!

OLD WOMAN 2: Good afternoon, Schoolmaster.

ICHABOD *(startled)*: Why, good afternoon, ladies.

KNICKERBOCKER: He was tall but lank with long arms and hands that dangled a mile out of his sleeves. His head was small with huge ears and a long nose.

OLD WOMAN 1: Will you be attending the Van Tassels' party tonight?

ICHABOD: That I will. I merely need to fetch my horse for the ride home.

OLD WOMAN 2: Well, you enjoy yourself, Schoolmaster. But be wary—there's mischief in the air.

STAGE DIRECTOR: Ichabod bows, then returns to his reading and whistling.

KNICKERBOCKER: Wary, indeed! It's said the Hollow is bewitched. The people are given to all kinds of marvelous superstitions . . . including the Legend of the Headless Horseman.

Scene 2: The Van Tassel's Estate

KNICKERBOCKER: Ichabod rode a broken-down plow horse. It was all skin and bones, and its tail was knotted with burrs. Still, it must have had some spark, for it went by the name of Gunpowder.

STAGE DIRECTOR: Ichabod dismounts in front of a huge estate.

KNICKERBOCKER: It was toward evening that Ichabod arrived at the Van Tassels'. He could not help but chuckle at the possibilities.

ICHABOD: Someday this may all be ours, Gunpowder! If only I can win the hand of Katrina Van Tassel!

KNICKERBOCKER: Katrina Van Tassel was as rosy-cheeked as one of her father's peaches. From the moment Ichabod laid eyes upon her, his only thought was how to gain her affections.

KATRINA: Good evening, Master Crane. Welcome to our home.

ICHABOD *(clearing his throat)***:** Why, thank you, Miss Katrina.

> **Think About It**
>
> What kind of person is Brom? How are he and Ichabod alike? How are they different?

KNICKERBOCKER: But Ichabod wasn't the only one interested in Katrina. Another was a burly, roaring hero of the countryside known as Brom Bones. Whenever a prank or brawl happened, the simple folk of Sleepy Hollow always shook their heads and guessed Brom Bones was at the bottom of it.

STAGE DIRECTOR: Brom Bones enters, strutting and pumping his chest.

BROM *(loudly)***:** Here I am, Katrina! What say you we go take a ride on Daredevil?

KATRINA *(giggling)***:** Don't be silly! Put Daredevil in the barn and come in the house. And don't act like such a brute!

BROM: Say, is that the schoolmaster's horse? What's he doing here? Come to give you singin' lessons?

KATRINA: The schoolmaster is an honored guest. What fun it is to have such a gentleman in our midst.

BROM: I don't know what you see in him. He's got dinner plates where his ears should be and shovels for feet.

KATRINA: You're just jealous.

BROM: Of him? Why, he looks like a scarecrow that's escaped the cornfield!

KNICKERBOCKER: Poor Ichabod. He would have had a pleasant life, if only his path had not been crossed by young Katrina!

> Knickerbocker's line gives a hint about the story's conflict. What do you think he means by it?

Scene 3: The Party

STAGE DIRECTOR: The guests gather in the great parlor.

VAN TASSEL: Welcome! Welcome to the party, everyone! Let the music and dancing begin!

ICHABOD: Dear Katrina, may I have this dance?

STAGE DIRECTOR: Katrina glances slyly at Brom.

KATRINA: Why, certainly, Master Crane.

Think About It

What does Katrina's glance suggest?

KNICKERBOCKER: Ichabod prided himself upon his dancing. Not a limb about his loosely hung body was still. But as he went clattering about the room with the beautiful Katrina, he was unaware that Brom Bones sat brooding in one corner.

BROM: I don't like this one bit.

STAGE DIRECTOR: The dance ends. Ichabod bows to Katrina then makes his way toward a group of older guests. They are sitting by the fire, telling marvelous tales of ghosts and goblins.

What significance do the names of the characters hold?

VAN AX: Many a ghost haunts the Hollow. There's the old Dutchman who walks the docks, shouting for a musket and a sword.

VAN RIPPER: And there's the woman in white, who haunts the dark glen at Raven Rock. To hear her shriek on a winter night before a storm is a bad omen.

OLD WOMAN 1: In these parts, Mr. Crane, you must take care to live a decent life. Those who don't run the risk of being carried away in the dead of night!

KNICKERBOCKER: All these tales, told in those drowsy whispers with which people talk in the dark, sank deep in the mind of Ichabod. This, in turn, caught the attention of Brom.

VANDERBLOOD: But, my friend, nothing we've told you rivals the Headless Horseman.

ICHABOD: The Headless Horseman?

OLD WOMAN 2: Yes, dear man. He is said to be the ghost of a soldier whose head had been carried away by a cannonball during the Revolutionary War. His ghost is often seen hurrying along in the darkness.

VAN AX: With the Horseman about, one doesn't dare to be caught upon the roadway during the witching hour.

VANDERBLOOD: His body is buried in the churchyard, and every night the ghost rides forth . . . in search of his head.

VAN RIPPER: He cannot rest until he finds it. The speed with which he rides is like a midnight blast. It's because he's in a hurry to get back to the churchyard before the light of day.

VANDERBLOOD: He's been seen several times of late, patrolling the hills. I myself have seen his horse tethered among the graves in the churchyard.

STAGE DIRECTOR: A decrepit old man interrupts the storytellers.

BROUWER: I didn't believe in the Horseman until one night last year. I met him in the road near the Old Tree. I suspect he was returning from his search, but I didn't know who he was. I called to him: "Show me your face, good man." He didn't answer, and when he turned there was nothing there—just the stump of a neck. Before I could react, he grabbed me by the shoulder and forced me to get up behind him.

STAGE DIRECTOR: The room is silent. The old man takes a bite out of his apple and chews it slowly.

ICHABOD: Wh-what happened next?

BROUWER: How we galloped! Over bush and brake, over hill and swamp . . . then we reached the bridge. That's when the Horseman suddenly turned into a skeleton, threw me into the brook, and sprang away over the treetops with a clap of thunder!

> **Think About It**
>
> The villagers' tales provide a clue to one of the themes of this play. What themes can you identify?

ICHABOD: Oh, my!

BROUWER: Oh, my, indeed! I will never forget it!

BROM: I'm not afraid of the Horseman. Ay, I too have seen him. I was returning one night from a neighboring village when he overtook me. Rather than give in to his terror, I offered to race him for a bowl of punch. That's right, a bowl of punch! And I would have won it too, but just as we came to the old church bridge, the Horseman vanished in a flash of fire.

KNICKERBOCKER: Ay, it was true. The old church bridge was surrounded by overhanging trees, which cast a gloom even in the daytime. It was the place the Headless Horseman was most frequently encountered, but it was also the place he could not pass.

BROM: If ever the Horseman comes after you, head for the bridge. If you can but reach that bridge, you are safe.

STAGE DIRECTOR: One by one, the guests depart, but hoping for a moment alone with Katrina, Ichabod is the last to leave.

> **Think About It**
>
> What do you think Ichabod wanted to talk to Katrina about? How do you think their conversation went?

Scene 4: The Ride Home

KNICKERBOCKER: It was midnight when a disappointed Ichabod finally departed, and all those stories of ghosts and goblins now came crowding upon his thoughts.

STAGE DIRECTOR: Ichabod trots along, flinching at every sound and shape.

KNICKERBOCKER: He remembered all too clearly the warnings of the townspeople.

VAN AX: One doesn't dare to be caught upon the roadway during the witching hour.

KNICKERBOCKER: The wind's howl became the woman in white.

VAN RIPPER: *Ohhhhwwww....* To hear her shriek on a winter night before a storm is a bad omen.

KNICKERBOCKER: A bullfrog croaking became the ghost of the Old Dutchman.

OLD WOMAN 1: *Crooaak!* Take care to live a decent life. Those who don't run the risk of being carried away in the dead of night!

STAGE DIRECTOR: Ichabod clutches tightly at Gunpowder's reins. To calm his nerves, he begins to whistle.

KNICKERBOCKER: His normally cheerful version of "Yankee Doodle" sounded like a funeral hymn. It was then he saw it: In the shadows on the edge of the road, something huge and misshapen towering above them.

VANDERBLOOD: Every night, the ghost rides forth in search of his head.

ICHABOD: *Gulp!...* What's to be done, Gunpowder?

KNICKERBOCKER: Every hair upon the schoolmaster's head stood on end.

ICHABOD: Wh-who-who ... are you? I-I-I say there, wh-who are y-y-you?

KNICKERBOCKER: The shadowy creature put itself in motion and stood at once in the middle of the road.

ICHABOD: *Gulp!* I s-s-say, sir, wh-wh-what is it you w-w-want with me?

KNICKERBOCKER: When there came no reply, Ichabod rained a shower of kicks upon Gunpowder, but the stranger whirled his horse to give chase.

ICHABOD: R-r-run, Gunpowder!

Think About It

Where are these people? Are they with Ichabod?

What's to be done? What would you do if you were Ichabod?

KNICKERBOCKER *(growing in intensity)*: As poor Ichabod glanced over his shoulder, he was horror-struck, for the man behind him was headless, and the head, which should have rested on his shoulders, was hanging from the pommel of the saddle!

ICHABOD: Fly, Gunpowder, fly!

KNICKERBOCKER: Away they dashed, stones flying and sparks flashing. Ichabod's flimsy garments fluttered in the air as he stretched his long, lank body over his horse's head. And suddenly, he remembered what Brom Bones had said.

BROM: If you can but reach that bridge, you are safe.

KNICKERBOCKER: Thundering forward, he heard the black steed close behind him.

ICHABOD: There it is, Gunpowder. The old church bridge!

KNICKERBOCKER: He whipped wildly in the air, spurring his horse onward.

ICHABOD: *Hyaw, hyaw!* Come on, Gunpowder!

KNICKERBOCKER *(most intensely)*: Gunpowder's hooves pounded upon the planks of the bridge. Ichabod cast a look behind, expecting the goblin to vanish in a clap of thunder . . . but instead he saw it rise up and hurl its head . . . at him!

ICHABOD: *Ahhhhhhhhhh!*

Epilogue

KNICKERBOCKER *(calmly now)*: The next morning, the old horse wandered home, but Ichabod never returned. A search led to the bridge. Along the bank of the brook, where the water ran dark and deep, Ichabod's hat was found and, close beside it, a shattered pumpkin. The brook was searched, but the body of the schoolmaster was nowhere to be found, leaving the good people to shake their heads and conclude that Ichabod Crane had been carried off . . . by the Headless Horseman of Sleepy Hollow.

Knickerbocker wants you to believe Ichabod was carried off, but how else can you explain his disappearance?

The Nose

by Nikolai Gogol (Russia, 1836)

Students will love performing Gogol's absurd Russian short story about a man who wakes up one morning to discover that his nose has fled his face. When he tracks it down, he finds that the Nose has become a government official and refuses to return to its rightful place. Imagine some young person dressed in a nose costume running around the stage! It's an unforgettable example of farce. The events in the story cannot be explained—though students may have a lot of fun trying. Be sure to talk about theme, setting, and conflict.

Storyteller 1

Storyteller 2

Ivan: The barber

Wife: Ivan's wife

Russian 1

Russian 2

Russian 3

Police Constable

Major Kovalyov: The Nose's rightful owner

Madame Nevsky: The maid

Nose: Yes, the Nose!

Clerk

Police Inspector

Doctor

Vocabulary				
bumbling	prominent	sniveling	kopeks	gallivanting
constable	crux	rubles	absurdities	culprit

Scene 1: The Barber's Home

STORYTELLER 1: A rather unusual bit of nonsense took place in Russia in 1836.

STORYTELLER 2: Ivan the Barber was cutting open his breakfast roll when he suddenly stopped.

IVAN: Wife, there seems to be something in my bread.

STORYTELLER 1: He probed at it with his knife.

IVAN: It's quite solid. What in the world could it be?

STORYTELLER 2: He stuck in his fingers and pulled out . . .

IVAN: A nose! Sure enough, it's a nose!

WIFE: You brute! You've gone and cut off someone's nose?

IVAN: It looks like Major Kovalyov's nose. I shave him every Wednesday.

WIFE: You buffoon! I have heard from three men this week that while shaving them you pulled their noses so hard they couldn't stand it. And now you've gone and pulled one right off!

IVAN: Stop, Wife! I'll wrap it up and set it in the corner for a while.

WIFE: As if I'm going to have a cut-off nose lying around the house! Oh, you old bungler! You blockhead! Get rid of it at once! And don't let the police catch you with it. They'll lock you up!

Scene 2: The Bridge

STORYTELLER 1: Ivan thought getting rid of a nose would be an easy task.

STORYTELLER 2: He planned on tossing it into the street, but he kept meeting people he knew.

RUSSIAN 1: Ivan, what are you doing bumbling around so early in the morning?

RUSSIAN 2: Ivan, who would want a shave from you at this hour?

RUSSIAN 3: Ivan, last week you did a poor job. I want this week's shave for free!

STORYTELLER 1: Finally, he managed to dump the package in the gutter.

STORYTELLER 2: Only to be spotted by a police constable.

> **Think About It**
>
> What is Ivan's standing in the community? Is he respected? How can you tell?

CONSTABLE: You, there! You've dropped something! Pick that up!

IVAN: Oh, my, that I have, sir. Thank you!

STORYTELLER 1: Ivan then walked to the bridge over the River Neva. He pretended to see if any fish was passing underneath, and then he tossed in the nose.

STORYTELLER 2: But there again was the constable.

CONSTABLE: You there, come here! What have you been doing on that bridge?

IVAN: I was just looking to see if there were any fish jumping.

CONSTABLE: You lie, brother. You won't get out of it like that!

IVAN: I tell you what: I'll shave you for free twice a week. Just let me go on my way.

CONSTABLE: That's rubbish! I already have three barbers to do that. Come with me.

Scene 3: Kovalyov's Apartment

STORYTELLER 1: Meanwhile, Major Kovalyov awoke and called to his maid.

KOVALYOV: Madame Nevsky, bring me a mirror and a basin.

STORYTELLER 2: Major Kovalyov was a proud man. He wore his government title, his starched shirts, and his prominent nose with great dignity.

MADAME NEVSKY *(gasping)***:** Oh, my!

KOVALYOV: What is it, woman? Has my pimple gotten worse?

MADAME NEVSKY: No, sir. There's no pimple. In fact, there's not even a nose! There's just a smooth patch where your nose should be. It's shaped kind of like a pancake.

What happened to the Major's nose? How is that possible?

KOVALYOV: No nose! What could have happened to it?

MADAME NEVSKY: You should pinch yourself, Major—to make sure you're awake!

KOVALYOV: That's a good idea, Madame Nevsky.

STORYTELLER 1: He pinched himself, but the nose remained absent.

KOVALYOV: Perhaps you should pinch me, Madame!

MADAME NEVSKY: Very well, sir.

STORYTELLER 2: And she did—hard, until Major Kovalyov cried out.

KOVALYOV: *Ouch!* Is it back? Is my nose where it is supposed to be?

MADAME NEVSKY: Why, no, sir. Just that flat patch that looks like a pancake.

KOVALYOV: What am I to do? What does one do when his nose has gone missing?

MADAME NEVSKY: Sounds like a job for the police.

KOVALYOV: Yes, the Police Inspector will surely be able to get to the crux of this.

STORYTELLER 1: So the Major hurried away to the police.

Think About It

What would you do if your nose disappeared?

Scene 4: The Street

KOVALYOV: What craziness this is! What could it all mean?

STORYTELLER 1: As the Major walked, he used a handkerchief to hide his face.

KOVALYOV: If only there had been something—*anything!*—to take the nose's place. That would be better than having nothing there at all!

STORYTELLER 2: Suddenly, he saw something for which there is no explanation.

STORYTELLER 1: Out of a carriage leapt a familiar form.

KOVALYOV *(aside)*: The hat, the sword—everything about it shows it is a Vice-Governor now. And yet I know it to be my own nose!

STORYTELLER 2: Major Kovalyov followed the Nose inside a building. To get the Nose's attention, he coughed and cleared his throat.

STORYTELLER 1: But the Nose ignored him.

KOVALYOV *(nervously)*: Uh, my good sir, I . . .

NOSE *(snottily)*: Yes, what is it you want?

KOVALYOV: Well, I think you should know your proper place a little better.

NOSE *(rudely)*: Pardon me, but I do not understand your meaning. What is it you're sniveling about?

KOVALYOV: Certainly you can understand how embarrassing it is for me to go around without a nose.

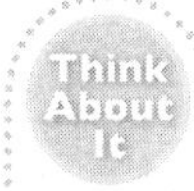

"What could it all mean?" speaks to one of the story's themes. What do you think the theme could be?

Think About It

"I understand nothing at all," says the Nose. This is an example of irony. Why is it humorous?

NOSE: I understand nothing at all. Explain yourself!

KOVALYOV: Isn't it plain to see? You are *my own* nose!

STORYTELLER 2: The Nose raised an eyebrow and glared at the Major.

NOSE *(snorting)***:** You speak in error. I am just myself, myself *separately*. In any case, there cannot have ever been any link between us for, judging from your uniform, you are of a rank much lower than I.

STORYTELLER 1: And the Nose turned his back to him.

KOVALYOV *(aghast, aside)***:** To be treated so snottily by my own nose! You, sir, are an imposter!

STORYTELLER 2: But the Nose had already dashed away.

Scene 5: The Newspaper Office

STORYTELLER 1: The Major headed for the newspaper office.

CLERK: One moment, please.

KOVALYOV: My dear sir, the matter is most pressing. Who do I see about placing an advertisement?

CLERK: One moment . . . two rubles, forty-three kopeks. Six rubles, four kopeks.

KOVALYOV: Sir, I insist! Fraud has been done, and I wish to offer a reward.

CLERK: What's the problem? Has your butler run off?

KOVALYOV: No, not my butler. It is my nose that is off!

CLERK: Nossov? Mister Nossov? What a strange name for a butler. Has this Mister Nossov stolen anything?

KOVALYOV: I said Nose, not Nossov. It is my nose that has disappeared. I think it is trying to make a fool of me.

CLERK: But how could a nose disappear?

KOVALYOV: I cannot explain it myself, but it is driving around the city in uniform, telling everyone it is a Vice-Governor. I beg you to print that anyone who can catch this Nose should return it to me immediately.

CLERK: Hmm. . . . A missing nose? Come now, I'm sorry but I can't print an advertisement like that. People will think our newspaper prints false tales and absurdities.

KOVALYOV: False tales? But it is the truth!

CLERK: Only last week there was a similar case. A lady said her poodle had run away, but in reality, it wasn't her poodle at all. It was her maid!

KOVALYOV: But I am not advertising about a lost poodle. It's my very own nose!

CLERK: All the same, I cannot print it.

KOVALYOV: Would it help if I let you see for yourself?

CLERK: Yes, I think it might. I've never seen anyone without a nose before!

STORYTELLER 2: The Major removed the handkerchief from his face.

CLERK: Strange, indeed. Very strange! It's like a newly fried pancake—a pancake right in the middle of your face there.

KOVALYOV: What a relief! Then you will print the ad?

CLERK: I don't see where that would help. You should hire a writer to tell your story, describing this as a freak of nature. Now that would grab some attention!

KOVALYOV: *Ugggbh!*

Think About It

Who is the main character in this story? What is his problem and what steps does he take to resolve his problem?

Scene 6: The Police Inspector's Office

STORYTELLER 2: Still holding the handkerchief over his face, the Major went straightaway to the Police Inspector.

KOVALYOV: Police Inspector, I need your help. My nose has taken leave of my face!

INSPECTOR: Just after supper is not the best time to call upon the Police Inspector. One should always rest after food, you know. Now, what is it you're babbling about?

KOVALYOV: My nose, sir. It has disappeared and is presumably parading about the city as a Vice-Governor! I saw it only a short while ago.

INSPECTOR: If you saw it only a short while ago, then it has not disappeared, has it? Besides, no one would steal the nose of a truly respectable man.

KOVALYOV: Sir!

INSPECTOR: Perhaps the Nose hasn't been stolen at all. Perhaps it has merely run away.

KOVALYOV: After such insults there is nothing further I wish to say to you! Good day!

Why are the Inspector's statements insulting to the Major?

Scene 7: Kovalyov's Apartment

STORYTELLER 1: Back at his apartment, Major Kovalyov paced to and fro.

KOVALYOV: What is a man without a nose?

MADAME NEVSKY: Nothing at all, if you ask me, sir.

KOVALYOV: It would have been better to have had it cut off in battle.

MADAME NEVSKY: At least, that would have been dignified, sir.

KOVALYOV: But as it is, my nose is gone, and I have nothing to show for it.

MADAME NEVSKY: Just a flat patch that looks a lot like a pancake.

KOVALYOV *(despairing)***:** Oh, what an absurd spectacle it is!

STORYTELLER 2: Suddenly, in strode the same police constable Ivan the Barber had encountered on the bridge.

CONSTABLE: I beg your pardon, sir, but have you lost a nose?

KOVALYOV: I have!

CONSTABLE: Then it is found. Curiously, I myself first took it for a gentleman. Lucky for you, I had my eyeglasses on, and I quickly recognized the "gentleman" was no gentleman at all. It was merely a nose! Apparently, it was gallivanting around like a Vice-Governor!

KOVALYOV: Where is the Nose now?

CONSTABLE: Don't worry. Knowing how much you'd be missing it, I brought it with me.

STORYTELLER 1: The police constable whistled, and in lumbered the Nose.

CONSTABLE: You'll find it's as good as ever. It is a curious fact that the culprit in this affair was that barber known as Ivan. I've long suspected him of trouble.

MADAME NEVSKY: Yes, that's your big old nose all right. I'd recognize that thing anywhere.

KOVALYOV:	Thank you, my good man! Thank you!
STORYTELLER 2:	The Major hugged the Nose and danced around the room with it.
MADAME NEVSKY:	But, how ever are you going to stick it back on?
STORYTELLER 1:	Suddenly worried, the Major frantically pressed the Nose into place on his face.
STORYTELLER 2:	But it would not stay put. It slumped to the floor, and when the Major went to pick it up again, it went stumbling around the room.
KOVALYOV:	Come, come, fool! Stop where you are! Madame Nevsky, send for the doctor! Quickly!
MADAME NEVSKY:	Right away, sir! Right away.
STORYTELLER 1:	When the doctor arrived, he viewed the Nose huddled in the corner and then examined the bare patch on the Major's face.
DOCTOR:	Hmm . . . let's have a look at this.
STORYTELLER 2:	Using his thumb and forefinger, he thumped the vacant patch with such force the Major cried out in pain.
DOCTOR:	I'm afraid it just won't do. I don't think you should risk further complications.
KOVALYOV:	What? Go about without a nose, only to have one crawling around my apartment like a pet, having to be fed and bathed, and . . . *and cleaned up after?*
DOCTOR:	I *could* stick it on again—I could do that easily—but I can assure you your troubles will only get worse.
KOVALYOV:	Things could not get any worse than they are now. Stick it on, I say, for how can I continue without a nose?!
DOCTOR:	Wash often in cold water, and, I assure you, you will be as healthy without a nose as with one. As for this Nose here, I will gladly take it off your hands. Gladly.
STORYTELLER 1:	At this, the Nose perked up and began to whimper.
KOVALYOV:	No, no! I would rather it were lost again!
DOCTOR:	Very well. I've done all I can here. I will send you the bill.

What lesson are you supposed to learn from this story?

Scene 8: Kovalyov's Apartment

STORYTELLER 1: The story of the Nose soon spread throughout the city.

STORYTELLER 2: Marvelous rumors were heard on every corner.

RUSSIAN 1: If you want to see it, it always takes a walk along the river around three o'clock.

Think About It

What's the setting of this particular scene?

RUSSIAN 2: I heard it has become an advisor to the Prime Minister.

RUSSIAN 3: No, that's not true at all. It has joined the ballet. I myself saw it perform Sunday night at the Royal Opera House.

RUSSIAN 2: The Royal Opera House? Since when can you afford to visit the Royal Opera House?

RUSSIAN 3: What's so absurd about that?

STORYTELLER 1: But farce really does occur in this world.

STORYTELLER 2: The Nose, which had briefly gone about the city as a Vice-Governor . . .

STORYTELLER 1: And more recently lived in a corner of the Major's apartment . . .

STORYTELLER 2: Suddenly found its proper place between Major Kovalyov's two cheeks.

KOVALYOV: What's this? Yes, my nose. Ha! Look, Madame Nevsky, surely there's a pimple on my nose!

MADAME NEVSKY: Neither a pimple nor a pancake, sir. Your nose is clear all over.

STORYTELLER 1: And it was at that moment that Ivan the Barber peeped round the door.

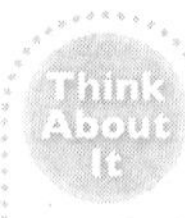

Why is the Major worried about whether Ivan's hands are clean?

IVAN *(timidly)***:** Good for a shave today, Major?

KOVALYOV: Tell me first whether your hands are clean.

IVAN: They are, sir.

KOVALYOV: Very well. But go *carefully*. After all, what man doesn't value his nose?

STORYTELLER 2: And from then on, Major Kovalyov gadded about the same as before.

STORYTELLER 1: And always the Nose accompanied him.

The Tell-Tale Heart

by Edgar Allan Poe (United States, 1843)

Clever formatting and careful structuring make Poe's masterpiece of terror and suspense perfect for the classroom. This is the story of a man who's lost his mind. When he imagines he hears the thumping of the Old Man's heart under the floorboards, his terrible crime is uncovered. While working on this play, consider reading aloud Poe's most famous work, "The Raven."

Cast of Characters

Raven Chorus: A flock of ranting ravens—or better yet, a murder of crows

Raven 1

Raven 2

Raven 3

Villainous Narrator: A madman and the teller of the tale

Old Man: Spends the entire play offstage or under the floorboards

The Old Man's Heart: Thump, thump!

Officer Edgar

Sergeant Allan

Constable Poe

Vocabulary

carriages, gargoyles, keen, suspicious, Darjeeling, morgues, villainous, taunted, shriek, hideous

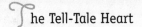

Scene 1 (*the only one!*)

RAVEN CHORUS *(flying in to land near the stage)***:** *Caw, caw, caw*...

RAVEN 1: Long before Goosebumps or Lemony Snicket...

RAVEN 2: Back in the day of horse-drawn carriages and candlelight...

RAVEN 3: The master of blood-curdling stories was a man named Edgar Allan Poe.

RAVEN 1: Poe wrote about murder and morgues...

RAVEN 2: About gargoyles and being buried alive...

RAVEN 3: And this tale—still considered one of the most horrific stories ever written.

RAVEN 1: It's the story of a man who has *lost his mind*...

VILLAINOUS NARRATOR *(sticking his head out from behind the curtains, interrupting)***:** WHAt? I'm NOT CrAzy! You mAy thINK I am, but I am nOt!

RAVEN CHORUS *(as the curtains open)***:** And thus the tale begins.

RAVEN 2: It starts with the Old Man.

VILLAINOUS NARRATOR *(calmly now)***:** Yes, that's right, the Old Man.

OLD MAN *(offstage, weakly)***:** Would you kindly bring me some tea?

VILLAINOUS NARRATOR: *(to the Old Man, cheerfully)***:** Of course! I'll be right there. With the morning paper, too.

OLD MAN *(offstage, kindly)***:** Thank you.... You don't look well today. Didn't you get any sleep last night?

VILLAINOUS NARRATOR *(offstage)***:** I am fine, Old Man. If anything, my senses are especially keen.

OLD MAN: You seem to have a headache. Let me get up and fix you something.

VILLAINOUS NARRATOR: No, no. You enjoy your tea.

RAVEN CHORUS: Such a kind-*hearted* old man.

The story's setting is in the past, but to the original readers, it would have been in the present. Would that have made it scarier?

What does the odd format of the narrator's words supposed to signify?

What is meant by the word *keen?*

VILLAINOUS NARRATOR:
*(returning to stage)***:** True enough. He had never done me harm. But he had this one sickly eye. How I hated to look at it! It was like that of a vulture. Pale blue with a milky white film upon it.

RAVEN CHORUS: A milky white film!

VILLAINOUS NARRATOR: I wasn't crazy! It was THE EYE! IT TAUNTED ME. IT BELITTLED ME! IT DROVE ME FROM THE ROOM! . . . I HAD TO EXTINGUISH THAT EYE!

RAVEN CHORUS: He had to extinguish THE EYE!

VILLAINOUS NARRATOR: So I set about the task. Night after night I crept into his room.

RAVEN CHORUS: He shone a light upon THE EYE.

VILLAINOUS NARRATOR: But every night, THE EYE was closed. . . . It was on the eighth night as I crept that I heard the Old Man sit up suddenly in bed.

RAVEN CHORUS: He cried out in fear.

OLD MAN *(offstage)***:** Who's there?!

VILLAINOUS NARRATOR: I remained still.

(silence)

For hours I stood without moving, barely breathing.

(silence)

And then I shone my light, a single beam upon THE EYE.

RAVEN CHORUS: It was open!

VILLAINOUS NARRATOR: WIDE, WIDE OPEN! And it made me furious to look upon that DULL BLUE MILKY EYE!

RAVEN CHORUS: The vulture's eye!

VILLAINOUS NARRATOR: And then I heard it.

RAVEN CHORUS: The beating of the old man's heart.

OLD MAN'S HEART: BUMP BUMP . . . BUMP BUMP . . . BUMP BUMP . . .

VILLAINOUS NARRATOR: FASTER and FASTER!

RAVEN CHORUS: LOUDER and LOUDER!

OLD MAN'S HEART: BUMP BUMP . . . BUMP BUMP . . . BUMP BUMP . . .

Think About It

The description of the eye shows that it disgusts the Narrator, but is there more to it than that? Why does the eye really bother him so much?

VILLAINOUS NARRATOR: I could stand it no longer! I leapt. *Ahhhhhhhhhhhhh!*

RAVEN CHORUS: *Ahhhhhhhhh!*

OLD MAN: *Ahhhhhhhhh!*

(silence)

RAVEN 1: It was over.

RAVEN 2: The heart was still.

RAVEN 3: THE EYE was closed forever.

VILLAINOUS NARRATOR: THE EYE would trouble me no more.

RAVEN 1: An hour later, there came a knock at the door.

RAVEN 2: BANG BANG BANG!

RAVEN 3: It was the police!

OFFICER EDGAR: There's been a complaint.

SERGEANT ALLAN: Your neighbors.

CONSTABLE POE: They called.

OFFICER EDGAR: A scream was heard.

SERGEANT ALLAN: Like this: *"Ahhhhhhh!"*

CONSTABLE POE: Yes, *"Ahhhhhhh!"*

OFFICER EDGAR: *"Ahhhhhh!"*

SERGEANT ALLAN: Or, at least, that's what they're saying.

CONSTABLE POE: It's suspicious, don't you think?

VILLAINOUS NARRATOR *(to the officers)***:** Yes, the shriek—a shriek of terror. It was my own . . . during a dream.

RAVEN CHORUS: Or a nightmare!

OFFICER EDGAR: May we come in?

SERGEANT ALLAN: Have a look around?

CONSTABLE POE: Investigate?

RAVEN CHORUS: He invited them in.

VILLAINOUS NARRATOR *(to the audience)***:** Yes, I invited them in. Would a crazy person have thought to do that? I wasn't worried, for I had carefully hidden the now CLOSED eye and SILENT heart beneath the floorboards!

OFFICER EDGAR: Who else lives here with you?

> **Think About It**
>
> What was different about the eighth night that prompted the Narrator to act?

SERGEANT ALLAN: Yes, with whom do you live?

CONSTABLE POE: And why isn't he here?

How are the Old Man's belongings significant?

VILLAINOUS NARRATOR *(to the officers)***:** Ah, the Old Man. He is . . . away. You see, there is his room. His bed is made. His belongings are in place.

OFFICER EDGAR: Is something wrong?

SERGEANT ALLAN: You seem to have a headache.

CONSTABLE POE: You should sit down.

VILLAINOUS NARRATOR: Yes, a fine idea. Perhaps you would join me for a spot of tea?

OFFICER EDGAR: A spot of tea?

SERGEANT ALLAN: Why, that would be lovely.

CONSTABLE POE: Yes, yes, a spot of tea.

RAVEN CHORUS: He served them tea.

VILLAINOUS NARRATOR *(to the audience)***:** Indeed! For what had I to fear? I brought chairs into the room and served the tea upon the very spot where I had replaced the floorboards.

OFFICER EDGAR: Ah, this is fine tea.

SERGEANT ALLAN: They say green tea is good for you, too.

CONSTABLE POE: But I'd have to say, Darjeeling is my personal favorite.

VILLAINOUS NARRATOR: The officers chatted about familiar things. It seems I'd fooled them well. Could a crazy man have done that?

Why won't they leave?

RAVEN CHORUS: But soon he wished them gone.

VILLAINOUS NARRATOR: I found myself growing pale. Why wouldn't they leave?

OFFICER EDGAR: Lots of strange things happening these days.

SERGEANT ALLAN: People acting strangely.

CONSTABLE POE: It's like there's something in the air.

VILLAINOUS NARRATOR: Then there came a ringing in my ears.

RAVEN CHORUS: A muffled, buzzing sound.

OLD MAN'S HEART: BUZZ, BUZZ, BUZZ . . . *(and continuing in background)*

VILLAINOUS NARRATOR: No doubt I grew very, very pale. I RAISED MY VOICE, but still they chatted.

OFFICER EDGAR: It must be nice to visit the countryside this time of year.

SERGEANT ALLAN: Yes, *peaceful*, I'd say.

CONSTABLE POE: What with the fall colors and all.

VILLAINOUS NARRATOR: The buzzing grew louder, until I realized it wasn't a buzzing at all, but a ticking sound.

RAVEN 1: Like that of a watch . . .

RAVEN 2: Or a clock . . .

RAVEN 3: Or a time bomb!

OLD MAN'S HEART: TICK TICK TICK TICK TICK . . . *(and continuing)*

VILLAINOUS NARRATOR: I paced to and fro, I clutched my forehead, but they chattered on as if nothing was wrong.

> Think About It
>
> Is this story realistic or unrealistic? What evidence supports your position?

OFFICER EDGAR: Getting out of the city to take a walk in the woods, why, it clears the mind.

SERGEANT ALLAN: Much like this tea.

CONSTABLE POE: Yes, green tea. It's good for the soul.

VILLAINOUS NARRATOR: The noise grew louder. And then, I knew it for what it was!

OLD MAN'S HEART: BUMP BUMP. BUMP BUMP. BUMP BUMP . . .

RAVEN CHORUS: LOUDER, LOUDER, LOUDER!

VILLAINOUS NARRATOR: Couldn't they hear it? I paced the floor with heavy strides. I hissed! I growled! I gestured with my arms!

OFFICER EDGAR: Anyway, why is it called Darjeeling?

SERGEANT ALLAN: I think it has something to do with where it's grown.

CONSTABLE POE: In India . . . unless I'm mistaken.

OLD MAN'S HEART: BUMP BUMP. BUMP BUMP. BUMP BUMP.

VILLAINOUS NARRATOR: And then it came to me. They were mocking me with their innocent smiles and their sips of tea!

RAVEN CHORUS: Oh, the agony!

OLD MAN'S HEART: BUMP BUMP. BUMP BUMP. BUMP BUMP.

OFFICER EDGAR: Well, all seems well here.

SERGEANT ALLAN: We should be reporting back at the station.

CONSTABLE POE: Thank you kindly for the tea, young man.

VILLAINOUS NARRATOR: LOUDER, LOUDER STILL! I could bear it no longer.

> Is there any evidence to suggest the police officers know something is amiss? Why does the Narrator believe they are mocking him?

RAVEN CHORUS: He could bear it no longer!

OLD MAN'S HEART: BUMP BUMP. BUMP BUMP. BUMP. . .

VILLAINOUS NARRATOR: Villains! Monsters! I did it! I confess! Tear up the floor! Here! Here! It is the BEATING OF HIS HIDEOUS HEART!

(silence)

VILLAINOUS NARRATOR *(suddenly flinging closed the curtains and scattering the ravens)***:** ThaT's riGht. I did it! But I sHan't tell you wHat haPpeneD neXt . . . nOr shall I tell you wHat's to haPpen noW, if you doN't stoP staring with those VULTURE EYES. . . .

What does happen next? Based on your knowledge of the Narrator and the facts from the story, what's your prediction? What does the author want you to think?

A Christmas Carol

by Charles Dickens (England, 1843)

This version of Dickens's famous story about Ebenezer Scrooge comes with a twist: It's Eleanora Scrooge who wakes on Christmas Eve and encounters the ghost of her long-dead business partner, Gladys Marley. It's "A Christmas Carol" with a female lead—an opportunity for an engaging compare-and-contrast lesson with the original text. This is also a great story for studying characterization and motivation.

Cast of Characters

Narrator 1

Narrator 2

Bob Cratchit: Scrooge's clerk

Ms. Eleanora Scrooge: A rich and cranky old banker

Elizabeth: Scrooge's cheerful niece

Old Lady Marley: Scrooge's dead business partner

Ghost Chorus: Ghostly sounds made by all the ghosts in unison

Ghost 1: The Ghost of Christmas Past

Ghost 2: The Ghost of Christmas Present

Ghost 3: The Ghost of Christmas Yet to Come (nonspeaking part)

Tiny Tina Cratchit: Bob's crippled daughter

Mrs. Cratchit: Bob's wife

Fezziwig: Scrooge's first employer

Passerby 1

Passerby 2

Boy

Other nonspeaking parts:

- **Buddy Lee**
- **Young Scrooge**

Vocabulary

niece, chamber, wander, massive, mourn, dreary, undigested, charity, toast, salary

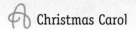

Scene 1: Christmas Eve, London

Think About It

Which words from the first few lines set the "mood" or "tone" of the play?

NARRATOR 1: You wouldn't think Christmas Eve to be a time for ghost stories, but here in the offices of Eleanora Scrooge and her long-dead partner, Gladys Marley, our ghostly tale begins.

NARRATOR 2: Let me say again that Old Lady Marley is dead. This you must understand.

CRATCHIT: Ms. Scrooge, ma'am, might I add some coal to the fire?

SCROOGE: Absolutely not! Coal costs money. Doesn't your coat keep you warm?

CRATCHIT: Not really, ma'am.

SCROOGE: Then I suggest you get a new one.

CRATCHIT: But, ma'am . . .

SCROOGE: That's enough, Mr. Cratchit! Back to work. There's money to be earned.

NARRATOR 1: Just as she did every Christmas, Scrooge's niece came visiting.

NARRATOR 2: She hoped to spread some cheer.

ELIZABETH: Merry Christmas, Auntie!

SCROOGE: Bah, humbug!

ELIZABETH: Christmas a humbug? You don't mean it!

SCROOGE: I do! What reason have you to be merry? You're not rich!

ELIZABETH: Come, dear Auntie. What reason have you to be so gloomy? You, with all your money? Where is your spirit?

SCROOGE: Bah, humbug! Christmas is nothing but a time of wasting money on things you don't need. If I had my way, every idiot who goes about saying "Merry Christmas" would be boiled in her own pudding.

ELIZABETH: Auntie!

SCROOGE: Niece! You celebrate Christmas your way. Let me celebrate it my way.

ELIZABETH: But you *don't* celebrate it.

SCROOGE: Let me not celebrate it then. But take my advice, it has done you no good.

Think About It

How do Scrooge's and Elizabeth's philosophies about life differ?

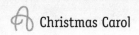

ELIZABETH: There are many things that do us good without making us rich. Though Christmas has never put a scrap of gold in my purse, I believe I am all the better for having celebrated it.

CRATCHIT: Yes, yes!

SCROOGE: Any more from you, Mr. Cratchit, and you'll celebrate Christmas by looking for a new job.

CRATCHIT: Yes, ma'am.

ELIZABETH: Don't be angry, Auntie. Have Christmas dinner with us tomorrow.

SCROOGE: Humbug!

ELIZABETH: But why not?

SCROOGE: That's enough! Good day, Niece.

ELIZABETH: So be it. But I shall keep my Christmas spirit till the end. Merry Christmas, Auntie! Merry Christmas, Mr. Cratchit!

CRATCHIT: Happy New Year, Elizabeth!

SCROOGE: Now there's a ridiculous notion: My clerk, with barely enough money to feed his family, and a crippled child too, talking about a happy new year. I must be mad!

Scene 2: Late That Same Evening

Think About It

"Darkness is cheap." How is this line important to the story?

GHOST CHORUS: *Owwooooh!*

NARRATOR 1: Darkness is cheap.

NARRATOR 2: It was while Scrooge sat by the fireplace in her dark and dreary house that she heard the door fly open . . .

NARRATOR 1: And the rattling of chains.

SCROOGE: It's humbug still! I won't believe it!

NARRATOR 2: Passing through the heavy door to Scrooge's chamber came a ghost with death-cold eyes.

NARRATOR 1: Its head was wrapped in bandages. It had chains locked around its body.

SCROOGE: *Pooh pooh!* I'm not a woman to be frightened by shadows.

MARLEY: You don't believe in me?

SCROOGE:	I don't! You're just an undigested bit of beef or an underdone potato. You're probably just a little stomach gas.
NARRATOR 2:	At this, the spirit raised a frightful cry and shook its chains with such an awful noise that Scrooge dropped to her knees and covered her face.
MARLEY:	*Owwooooh!*
SCROOGE:	Mercy, dreadful spirit! What is it you want with me?
MARLEY:	Much! In life I was your partner, Gladys Marley. I am doomed to forever drag this chain and wander through the world. Oh, woe is me!
SCROOGE:	But why are you chained?
MARLEY:	I drag the chain I made while living. Each link is a kind deed I didn't do or a favor I left undone. This time of year, I suffer most. Oh, why did I walk through crowds of needy people but not show charity?!
SCROOGE:	But you were always such a good businesswoman, Gladys.
NARRATOR 1:	Again the ghost raised a cry and shook its chains.
MARLEY:	*Owwooooh!* Mankind should have been my business. I should have dealt in mercy and kindness! Do you know the weight of the chain *you're* making, Eleanora? It was as long as mine seven Christmas Eves ago. Imagine how massive it is now!
SCROOGE:	Gladys, what can be done?
MARLEY:	Hear me, Scrooge! You have a chance to escape my fate. You will be haunted by three spirits. They are your only hope to change your future. Expect the first when the clock strikes 1.
GHOST CHORUS:	*Owwooooh!*

What does the chain represent? How massive would Scrooge's be?

Scene 3: One O'Clock, Past Midnight

NARRATOR 1:	As the clock struck 1, Scrooge awoke to find an eerie visitor.
GHOST 1:	I am the Ghost of Christmas Past. Rise and walk with me.
NARRATOR 2:	They passed magically into Scrooge's past.
GHOST 1:	Do you know this place?

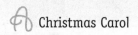

SCROOGE: Know it? I held my first job here! Why, look, it's old Fezziwig. Bless her heart!

NARRATOR 1: Ms. Fezziwig looked at the clock and clapped her hands.

FEZZIWIG: It's Christmas Eve! Yo, ho, there, young Eleanora! Yo, ho, everyone! No more work tonight. Clear the floor for dancing and singing and celebrating Christmas!

NARRATOR 2: Food was brought in. The music began. Everyone started dancing—including young Scrooge.

GHOST 1: Such a waste of money, all this.

SCROOGE: A waste of money?

GHOST 1: Isn't it?

SCROOGE: Of course not! Look how happy everyone is. Fezziwig was a master at making people happy. She did little things mostly. It was the way she looked at you, or a pat on the back. And this dancing!

> **Think About It**
> Why does the ghost say the party is a waste of money? How does Scrooge's response show how her attitude might be changing?

GHOST 1: Who are you dancing with?

SCROOGE: Ah, Buddy. It's young Buddy Lee.

GHOST 1: You loved him, but you didn't marry him.

SCROOGE: I first needed to seek my fortune.

GHOST 1: You mean, there was no profit in loving him!

SCROOGE: Spirit, why do you torture me? Show me no more. I don't wish to see it!

> **Think About It**
> Was Scrooge wrong to have put off marrying? How would her life have been different?

Scene 4: Two O'Clock, Past Midnight

GHOST CHORUS: *Owwooooh!*

GHOST 2: Wake up, lady! Wake up and know me better!

NARRATOR 1: The second spirit was as grand and joyful as the season.

NARRATOR 2: Its eyes were clear and kind, yet they frightened Scrooge.

GHOST 2: I am the Ghost of Christmas Present. I'll bet you've never seen anything like me before!

SCROOGE: Spirit, take me where you will. Let me learn from it.

> **Think About It**
> The author intended for this ghost to remind you of someone. Who?

GHOST 2:	Off with us then! Touch my robe!
SCROOGE:	Where are we?
GHOST 2:	You don't know the house of your own clerk, Bob Cratchit?
SCROOGE:	Is this his house? He does pretty well, considering how little I pay him.
GHOST 2:	Is that so? Come inside. The family is just now sitting down for Christmas dinner.
TINY TINA:	Mother, there never was such a grand goose as this!
CRATCHIT:	Splendid, my dear. It's wonderful!
SCROOGE:	So excited over a little goose! You'd think it was a prize turkey.
GHOST 2:	It's all they can afford! They're poor!
SCROOGE:	True, but they're happy. Look how pleased they are with one another—especially that Tiny Tina.
CRATCHIT:	A toast! To Ms. Scrooge, the founder of our feast!
MRS. CRATCHIT *(angrily)***:**	The founder of our feast, indeed! I wish she were here now. I'd give her a piece of my mind to feast upon!
CRATCHIT:	My dear! It's Christmas. Let's not be angry.
MRS. CRATCHIT:	I'll toast her health because it's Christmas, but that's all. Long life to her! Merry Christmas to that nasty, unfeeling, unkind founder of our feast, Ms. Scrooge.
ALL:	Merry Christmas!
TINY TINA:	And God bless us, everyone!
SCROOGE:	Tiny Tina looks so frail! Tell me, Spirit, will she live?
GHOST 2:	I see an empty seat at the table. I see a tiny crutch with no owner.
SCROOGE:	Oh, no! Say she will be spared!
GHOST 2:	If things remain the same, the child will die.
GHOST CHORUS:	*Owwooooh!*

This is a critical point in the story. Why?

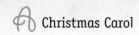

Scene 5: Three O'Clock, Past Midnight

NARRATOR 1: The third ghost was hidden inside a black robe. It left nothing visible save for one crooked hand.

SCROOGE: You are the Ghost of Christmas Yet to Come?

NARRATOR 2: The spirit didn't answer. It merely pointed its long, bony finger into a weed-infested churchyard.

SCROOGE: Whose funeral is this? Why is no one here to mourn? Tell me, Spirit, is there anyone in this town who cared for this person?

PASSERBY 1: When did she die?

PASSERBY 2: Last week.

PASSERBY 1: What was the matter with her?

PASSERBY 2: An empty heart, I suppose.

PASSERBY 1: Her money didn't do her much good, did it?

PASSERBY 2: Not a single person here to mourn her!

PASSERBY 1: But think of all the money she saved with such a cheap funeral!

PASSERBY 2: Ha, ha, ha!

NARRATOR 1: The ghost pointed Scrooge to a gravestone.

SCROOGE: Before I look, Spirit, tell me one thing. Can this future be changed?

NARRATOR 2: The Spirit gave no reply. Scrooge trembled. She looked upon the stone and read the words, *ELEANORA SCROOGE.*

GHOST CHORUS: *Owwooooh!*

SCROOGE *(sobbing)***:** No, Spirit! Hear me! I am not the person I was! I will honor Christmas in my heart! I will celebrate it all year long. Please tell me I can still erase the name upon this stone!

> **Think About It**
>
> Because of Scrooge's encounters with the ghosts, this story appears to be unrealistic. Is there any way it could be viewed as realistic?

Scene 6: Christmas Morning

NARRATOR 1: When Scrooge awoke, she was so happy to see daylight, she laughed out loud. For a woman who had been out of practice for so long, it was a wonderful laugh.

NARRATOR 2: She opened her window and called to a boy.

SCROOGE: What day is it, my fine fellow?

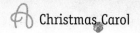

BOY: Today? Why, it's Christmas Day!

SCROOGE: I haven't missed it then! Listen, my young fellow. You know the prize turkey hanging in the butcher's window?

BOY: The one that's bigger than me?

SCROOGE: Yes, that one. I'll pay you to go and buy it and have it brought here. If you come back in less than five minutes, I'll pay you double!

BOY: Yes, ma'am! Merry Christmas, ma'am!

SCROOGE: I'll have it delivered to Bob Cratchit's. Then I must join my niece for dinner. Heaven be praised, I haven't missed it!

Scene 7: The Next Day

NARRATOR 1: The next morning, Scrooge arrived at the office early. She wanted to catch Bob Cratchit reporting late!

SCROOGE: Mr. Cratchit, you're eighteen and a half minutes late!

CRATCHIT: It's only once a year, ma'am. We were making merry rather long last night. It won't happen again.

SCROOGE: I'll tell you what, Cratchit. I'm not going to stand for this any longer!

NARRATOR 2: Poor Bob Cratchit! He was certain he was about to be fired.

SCROOGE: And therefore, Mr. Cratchit . . . I'm doubling your salary!

NARRATOR 1: Cratchit was stunned!

SCROOGE: Merry Christmas, Bob! The merriest Christmas ever! And your salary is just a start. I'll help your struggling family any way I can. And Tina, whatever she needs, I'll buy it. Now, let's warm up this place. Buy some more coal, Bob Cratchit. Before you dot another *i*, buy more coal.

Stories are often defined by how the main character changes. How and why has Scrooge changed?

NARRATOR 2: Scrooge was better than her word. She became as good a person and as good a friend as the city knew.

NARRATOR 1: It was always said, if anyone knew how to celebrate Christmas, it was Eleanora Scrooge.

NARRATOR 2: May that be said of all of us.

TINY TINA: And God bless us, everyone!

The Necklace

by Guy de Maupassant (France, 1884)

Maupassant the Cat and Flaubert the Mouse tell the exasperating tale of the discontented Matilda Loisel, a young French woman who takes her happiness for granted and consequently trades it all for a fake diamond necklace. Students consistently rank this among their favorites to perform. It's a great story to talk about irony, plot, and moral. What is the lesson for us all?

Maupassant *(MO-puh-sont)***:** The cat

Matilda Loisel *(LWA-zel)*

Marie-Claire: The maid

Monsieur Loisel *(meh-sewr LWA-zel)***:** Matilda's husband

Flaubert *(FLO-bare)***:** The mouse

Madame Forestier *(FOR-es-tee-ay)***:** Matilda's friend

Madame Ambassador: The ambassador's wife

The Ambassador

Vocabulary

discontent
wealthy
affair
elegant

franc (fronk): French currency
Tais-toi! (tay-TWA): Be quiet!
bon chic (bon-SHEEK): very hip
C'est vrai (say-VRAY): It's true

waltzed
content

Scene 1: Chez Loisel

MAUPASSANT *(arrogantly)*: Oh, hello there. Or shall I say, *bonjour.* After all, we are in Paris. My name is Maupassant. As you can see, I am a cat. I live here with Madame Loisel, a young lady as charming as she is discontent. . . . Ah, here she comes now.

MATILDA *(seeming distressed)*: Oh, Maupassant, you're the only thing of value in this whole house! Marie-Claire? Marie-Claire!

MARIE-CLAIRE: *Oui,* Madame.

MATILDA: Maire-Claire, do try to straighten up before the master gets home. Everything looks so shabby!

MARIE-CLAIRE: But, Madame, you have such a beautiful home.

MATILDA: Nothing but faded wallpaper and worn furniture. How it tortures me to live here!

MAUPASSANT: As I was saying, Madame is a charming young lady. But she has rich tastes.

MATILDA: Make it better, Marie-Claire.

MARIE-CLAIRE: Madame?

MATILDA: Dust, Marie-Claire! Straighten! Fluff!

MARIE-CLAIRE: Yes, Madame. Right away, Madame.

MAUPASSANT: Unfortunately, Madame is about to learn a hard lesson. It seems that what's least important in life is often the most costly. Wait, here comes Monsieur Loisel. Madame wishes he were royalty or wealthy. He is neither, but tonight he has a gift for her.

LOISEL: Dear Matilda, have I a surprise for you!

MATILDA: What's this?

LOISEL: It's an invitation to the Ambassador's Ball. I went to a great deal of trouble to get it.

MATILDA *(suddenly angry)*: What would I want with this?

LOISEL: But I thought it would make you happy. You never go out—and this is such a big event! Everyone important will be there.

MATILDA: What do you think I have to wear to such a fancy affair?

Think About It

Already the author has identified the source of the story's conflict or problem. Can you identify it?

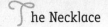

LOISEL: Why . . . how about that dress you wear to the theater? It's pretty enough.

MATILDA: The dress I wear to the theater? The dress I wear to the theater?! Are you mad?

> **Think About It**
>
> What is meant by the word *mad* in this line?

LOISEL: But what's the matter? Please don't cry, Matilda. What's wrong?

MATILDA: Nothing . . . only I can't go because I have nothing to wear. Give the invitation to someone whose wife is better dressed than I.

LOISEL *(after a pause)***:** Don't be sad, Matilda. How much would a nice outfit cost—something elegant?

MATILDA: Well . . . I don't know exactly. I should think four hundred francs ought to do it.

LOISEL *(after another pause)***:** Very well. I will give you four hundred francs. But do try to get a dress you'll be happy with.

MAUPASSANT: Poor Loisel. He looks a little pale.

Scene 2: Chez Loisel

FLAUBERT: Wait a minute! You mean to tell me . . .

MAUPASSANT: This is Flaubert, everyone. Flaubert, if Madame caught sight of you, she'd jump up and down screaming until Marie-Claire came and smashed you to bits with her dust mop.

FLAUBERT: *Dust mop, smush mop!* Now listen, Maupassant. You mean to tell me that Monsieur Loisel is going to empty his savings and work overtime just so Matilda can buy a dress?

MAUPASSANT: We're already in Scene 2, Flaubert, so I suspect he already has.

FLAUBERT: Does he honestly think a new dress will make her happy?

MAUPASSANT: Why wouldn't it?

FLAUBERT: Because she . . .

MAUPASSANT: Shhh. *Tais-toi,* Flaubert! They're coming.

MARIE-CLAIRE: Oh, my, Madame! You look . . . you look . . .

MAUPASSANT: I believe the phrase she's looking for is *bon chic*—very hip.

> Who is the story's main character—Matilda or Loisel? Why do you think so?

LOISEL: Stunning, my dear!

MATILDA: Something's not right.

FLAUBERT *(from under the sofa)***:** I knew it.

MARIE-CLAIRE: Madame?

LOISEL: But what could be wrong?

MATILDA *(suddenly crying)***:** Oh, no. Oh, no! What am I to do?

LOISEL: What is it, Matilda?

MATILDA: I haven't any jewelry! Not a single stone with which to adorn myself. I shall look so poor!

LOISEL: You can wear some flowers. They're very *chic* this time of year.

MATILDA: How embarrassing it would be to appear so shabby in the midst of rich women. No, I can't go.

FLAUBERT: Can she still return the dress?

LOISEL: I have it. We're so silly. Call on your friend, Madame Forestier! She will certainly lend you some jewels.

MATILDA: *C'est vrai!* I hadn't thought of that. Come, Maupassant. We must go at once!

Scene 3: Chez Forestier

MATILDA: Oh, Maupassant, I do so hope Madame Forestier takes pity on me.

FORESTIER: Why, Matilda, how nice to see you! And you've brought Maupassant! What a handsome animal!

MAUPASSANT *(while being scratched)***:** Yes, yes, it's true! Under the chin, please!

Think About It

To whom is Maupassant speaking in this line? What does it sound like to Madame Forestier and Matilda?

FORESTIER: What brings you here, Matilda?

MATILDA: It seems I've been invited to the Ambassador's Ball. Dear Monsieur Loisel has gone out of his way to get me an invitation and buy me a new dress.

FORESTIER: Oh, my. The Ambassador's Ball! You must be thrilled!

MATILDA: Yes . . . and no. I'm ashamed to say I haven't any jewelry to wear. Monsieur Loisel means well, but after all, he's only a clerk. May I borrow some jewelry from you?

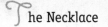

FORESTIER: Why, of course you can! Look, here's my case.

MATILDA: *Oh là là!* However will I choose? There are so many wonderful pieces!

FORESTIER: Just trinkets, my dear.

MAUPASSANT: Matilda and a case full of jewels? This could take awhile, so allow me to advance the story. It seemed nothing in Madame Forestier's case satisfied Matilda's tastes . . . until she discovered the necklace. Her heart skipped a beat. Her hands trembled.

> **Think About It**
>
> Why would it take awhile? What does it say about Matilda's character?

MATILDA: Could you lend me this diamond necklace? Only this?

FORESTIER: Certainly! Now go enjoy the Ambassador's Ball!

Scene 4: The Ambassador's Ball

FLAUBERT: So how'd she make out?

MAUPASSANT: Quite well, in fact.

FLAUBERT: So she's going to the ball?

MAUPASSANT: She's already there.

FLAUBERT *(suddenly seeing)*: Oh, wow, look at that! Look at the tails on that guy! Wealth, power, beauty—it's all here, isn't it? But how did I get here?

> Is this story realistic or unrealistic? Can it be both?

MAUPASSANT: You're not here. You're merely telling the story.

FLAUBERT: Really?! Well, then, so Matilda goes to the ball . . .

MADAME: And who's this elegant young lady?

LOISEL: Ambassador, Madame, I'd like you to meet my wife, Matilda.

MADAME: What a lovely smile you have. Come, darling, let me show you around.

AMBASSADOR: That's a fine lady you have there, young man. The prettiest thing here!

FLAUBERT: So, she's a hit!

MAUPASSANT: Of course she was. The necklace sparkled. Madame Ambassador showed her off as if she was her own daughter. Everyone wanted to dance with her. It was 4 a.m. before Monsieur could convince her to leave.

MATILDA: We must hurry out, dear husband, before someone sees my coat.

LOISEL: No one will notice your coat, Matilda.

MATILDA: All the other women are wearing furs, whereas mine is old and out of fashion. Please, let's hurry.

LOISEL: At least let me call you a cab. It's chilly out.

MATILDA: But we'll be noticed. We can walk down the street. A cab will happen by sooner or later.

LOISEL: Very well, my dear. If only to keep up appearances.

Scene 5: Chez Loisel

FLAUBERT: I don't see what the big deal is. She goes to the ball. She has a great time. End of story.

MAUPASSANT: Not quite, Flaubert. There is still that lesson to be learned.

LOISEL: I thought we'd never find a cab. I'm still shivering.

MATILDA: Oh, but it was worth it. What a splendid evening! Madame Ambassador was so wonderful. And, did you know, I waltzed with the Ambassador?

LOISEL: I'm glad you enjoyed yourself, Matilda, but I still have to report to work in the morning.

MATILDA: Just one more look.

MAUPASSANT: That's when Matilda stepped in front of the mirror one last time.

MATILDA: Oh, no! The necklace . . . Madame Forestier's diamond necklace . . . it's gone!

LOISEL: What? How's that? Are you sure you had it when we left the ball?

MATILDA: Yes, I felt it as we came out.

LOISEL: I will go out and look for it.

MAUPASSANT: Loisel searched the streets. Later that day, he went to the cab offices. He put an ad in the newspaper and offered a reward.

FLAUBERT: Did he find it? Did he find the necklace?

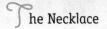

MATILDA: Darling, I'm so glad your home! Tell me you found it!

LOISEL *(sadly)*: Write your friend. Tell her you must have the clasp on the necklace repaired. That might give us time to find a replacement.

Scene 6: La Rue

FLAUBERT: A replacement? They can't afford a replacement. A necklace like that?

MAUPASSANT: After a great deal of shopping, they found a necklace that seemed to them exactly like the one they had lost. But it was very expensive.

FLAUBERT: Go ahead. Give me the bad news.

MAUPASSANT: Thirty-six thousand francs. True, they couldn't afford it. So they borrowed the money, and then spent ten years paying it back. They fired the maid.

MARIE-CLAIRE *(exiting, bawling)*: *Boo, hoo, hoo . . .*

FLAUBERT: Not Marie-Claire! Oh, how I loved that old woman!

MAUPASSANT: They moved to a truly shabby, one-room apartment. Loisel found a second job at night. Even Matilda took in work as a washwoman.

FLAUBERT: They went on like that for ten years?

MAUPASSANT: What else could they do? Just after making the final payment, Matilda bumped into Madame Forestier.

MATILDA: Madame Forestier! Good morning.

FORESTIER: Do I know you?

MATILDA: It's me, Matilda!

FORESTIER: My poor Matilda! How you've changed.

MATILDA: It's true. I've had some hard times—and all because of you.

FORESTIER: Because of me? Whatever do you mean?

MATILDA: You recall the necklace you loaned me? Well, I lost it.

FORESTIER: But you returned it to me.

The story's conflict centers around the lost necklace. What do the characters do to resolve this conflict?

Why doesn't Madame Forestier recognize Matilda?

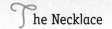

MATILDA: I returned another exactly like it. It has taken us ten years to pay for it. You can understand how hard it's been for us to live in poverty for so long, but it is finally finished, and I am decently content.

Compare this line to the very first line of the play. How has Matilda changed? How is it an example of irony?

FORESTIER: You say you bought a necklace to replace mine? My poor Matilda. Had you only come to me. My diamonds were false. They weren't worth but five hundred francs.

FLAUBERT *(after a pause)***:** Boy, that is a hard lesson.

MAUPASSANT: Indeed, Flaubert. Indeed. A lesson for all of us.

What is the lesson or moral of the story? What are we supposed to have learned?

Rikki-Tikki-Tavi

by Rudyard Kipling (England, 1894)

This is Kipling's story of a heroic young mongoose that saves an English family from a pair of vengeful cobras. Originally from *The Jungle Book*, it gives young people an introduction to British-occupied India and young actors the opportunity to experiment with characterization. It's a good story for looking at "perspective." Consider incorporating flutes (recorders) into the beginning and end of the snake charmers' narration.

Snake Charmer 1

Snake Charmer 2

Teddy: An English boy living in India

Alice: Teddy's mother

Big Man: Teddy's father

Rikki-Tikki-Tavi: A heroic mongoose

Darzee: A songbird

Deezar: Another songbird, Darzee's wife

Nag: A hooded king cobra

Nagaina: Another hooded king cobra, Nag's wife

Chuchundra: The fearful muskrat

Chorus: Darzee and others

Vocabulary	bungalow	roaming	triumph	tuft	brood
	curiosity	stealthily	valiant	scuttled	quivered

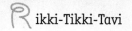

Scene 1: A Bungalow in India

What is the setting of this story?

SNAKE CHARMER 1: This is the story of the great war Rikki-tikki-tavi fought throughout the rooms and garden of a big bungalow in India.

SNAKE CHARMER 2: When Rikki-Tikki was very young, a flood washed him out of his burrow and carried him down a ditch to the middle of a garden.

TEDDY: Look, Mother, here's a dead mongoose. We should give him a proper funeral.

ALICE: Perhaps he isn't really dead, Teddy. Let's dry him off.

BIG MAN: He's not dead—just half choked. Now don't frighten him, and we'll see what he'll do once he's warmed up a bit.

SNAKE CHARMER 1: Soon Rikki was himself again and, like all mongooses, he was eaten up with curiosity.

SNAKE CHARMER 2: The mongoose motto is "Run and find out," so within moments Rikki had run around the entire room, and then he jumped on the boy's shoulder.

BIG MAN: Don't be frightened, Teddy. That's how he makes friends.

TEDDY: *Ouch!* He's tickling me.

RIKKI: *Rikk-tikk-tikki!*

ALICE: Good gracious, he's a wild creature! I suppose he's tame only because we've been kind to him.

BIG MAN: Every mongoose is like that. As long as Teddy doesn't pick him up by the tail, he'll run in and out of the house all day long.

RIKKI *(aside)***:** There is much to find out about this family. I shall certainly *stay* and find out.

SNAKE CHARMER 1: Rikki spent all that day roaming the house.

SNAKE CHARMER 2: And when Teddy went to bed, Rikki-tikki climbed up, too.

ALICE: I don't like that. He may bite the child.

BIG MAN: He'll do no such thing. Having a mongoose around is the surest way to protect against deadly snakes. Why, if one came into the room right now . . .

ALICE: *Shhh!* I don't want to think of anything so awful. Snakes are the one thing I hate about India.

SNAKE CHARMER 1: And well she should, for a cobra inside the garden walls brings danger and death.

Scene 2: The Bungalow Garden

SNAKE CHARMER 1: The next morning, Rikki met Darzee, the songbird, sitting on the edge of his nest, crying softly.

RIKKI: What is the matter?

DARZEE: Yesterday, one of our babies fell out of the nest, and Nag ate him.

RIKKI: That is terrible! Who is this Nag?

NAG: *Hissss.* Who is Nag? I am Nag. *Hissss*... look, and be afraid!

SNAKE CHARMER 2: Out from the brush came a huge cobra, spreading its massive hood.

> **Think About It**
>
> Thus begins the conflict. What is the conflict in this story?

SNAKE CHARMER 1: Rikki knew a cobra's business is death.

SNAKE CHARMER 2: But a mongoose can't stay frightened for long. Rikki knew a mongoose's business is to fight snakes.

RIKKI: Well, cobra or no cobra, do you think it is right for you to eat baby birds?

SNAKE CHARMER 1: Nag watched the grass behind Rikki, hoping to catch Rikki off his guard.

NAG: *Hissss*... let us talk. You eat eggs. Why shouldn't I eat birds?

> **Think About It**
>
> If Rikki eats eggs, why shouldn't Nag eat birds? If you were Rikki, how would you answer this question?

DEEZAR: Behind you! Look behind you.

SNAKE CHARMER 2: Rikki jumped up in the air as the head of Nagaina, Nag's terrible wife, whizzed past below him.

NAG: *Hiss.* Wicked, wicked birds!

SNAKE CHARMER 1: Rikki's eyes grew red and hot. He sat back on his tail and hind legs and chattered with rage.

RIKKI: *Rikk-tikk-tikki!*

SNAKE CHARMER 2: But Nag and Nagaina disappeared into the grass.

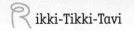

Scene 3: The Garden and Bungalow, at Night

SNAKE CHARMER 1: That night, Rikki went out in the dark and bumped into Chuchundra, the muskrat.

CHUCHUNDRA *(whimpering)*: *Errh,* please don't hurt me, Rikki-tikki!

RIKKI: Why would a snake-hunter hurt a muskrat?

CHUCHUNDRA: *Errh,* how am I to be sure some dark night Nag won't mistake me for you?

RIKKI: I will take care of Nag.

CHUCHUNDRA: *Errh,* but those who kill snakes get killed by snakes. Then what? Nag is everywhere, Rikki-tikki.

RIKKI: What do you mean by that?

CHUCHUNDRA: *Errh,* I mustn't tell you anything, but can't you hear, Rikki-tikki?

SNAKE CHARMER 2: Rikki listened. He could just catch the faintest *scratch-scratch* of a snake on brickwork.

RIKKI: That's Nag or Nagaina crawling into one of the bathrooms!

SNAKE CHARMER 1: Rikki stole off to the bathroom in the bungalow.

SNAKE CHARMER 2: At the bottom of the wall, there was a brick pulled out for the pipes. Rikki listened. On the other side, Nag and Nagaina were whispering.

NAGAINA: *Hisss.* Go in quietly. Remember that the Big Man is the first one to bite. Then we will hunt for Rikki-tikki together. *Hisss . . .*

NAG: *Hisss.* Are you sure there is something to be gained by attacking the people?

NAGAINA: When the house is emptied of people, Rikki will have to go away, and we will rule the garden. *Hisss.* When our eggs hatch, our young snakes will need room and quiet.

SNAKE CHARMER 1: Rikki tingled with rage. Then he saw Nag's head come stealthily through the hole.

RIKKI *(aside)*: If I strike him here, Nagaina will know, but if I fight him on the open floor, the odds are in his favor. What am I to do?

How does the character of Rikki compare to the character of Chuchundra? How is Chuchundra's character important to the story?

> **Think About It**
> How is the water jar a clue to the story's time setting?

SNAKE CHARMER 2: Nag waved to and fro, and then Rikki heard him drinking from the big water jar that was used to fill the bath.

NAG: Ah, that is good. *Hissss.* Now, I shall wait here till the Big Man comes in the morning. Nagaina, do you hear me? I shall wait here in the cool till daytime. Then I will strike.

SNAKE CHARMER 1: There was no answer from outside, so Rikki knew Nagaina had gone away.

SNAKE CHARMER 2: Nag hid by the water jar, but Rikki stayed still. After an hour, he began to move, muscle by muscle, toward the jar.

RIKKI: At last, Nag is asleep. I must aim for the head, and once I am there, I must not let go. O, Rikki!

CHORUS:
At the hole where he went in
Red-Eye called to Wrinkle-Skin.
Hear what little Red-Eye saith:
Nag, come up and dance with death!

RIKKI: *Rikk-tikk-tikki!*

SNAKE CHARMER 1: Rikki jumped. He bit and held on. He was battered to and fro as a rat is shaken by a dog, but he did not let go.

SNAKE CHARMER 2: The noise of Rikki being thrown about the bathroom woke the family. The Big Man came in with his gun, but Nag was already dead.

BIG MAN: It's the mongoose again, Alice. The little chap has saved our lives now.

RIKKI: I must get some rest if I am to settle with Nagaina. She will be worse than five Nags, and there's no knowing when her eggs will hatch.

> **Think About It**
> Why is Rikki worried about Nagaina's eggs hatching?

Scene 4: The Garden, the Next Morning

SNAKE CHARMER 1: In the morning, news of Nag's death was all over the garden. Darzee chirped a song of triumph at the top of his voice.

DARZEE:
Who hath delivered us, who?
Tell me his nest and his name.
Rikki, the valiant, the true,
Tikki, with eyeballs of flame . . .

RIKKI: You silly tuft of feathers! Is this any time to sing?

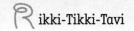

DARZEE: *Give him the Thanks of the birds,*
Bowing with tail-feathers spread!
Praise him with nightingale-words,
Nay, I will praise him instead.

RIKKI: Are you listening to me, Darzee?

DARZEE: Nag is dead! He will never eat our babies again.

RIKKI: That's true enough, but what about Nagaina?

DARZEE: Nagaina called for Nag, but the Big Man tossed him upon the rubbish heap. Let us sing about the great, the red-eyed Rikki-tikki!

Who hath delivered us, who?...

Is this story realistic or unrealistic? How do you know?

RIKKI: Stop singing a minute, Darzee. You're safe enough in your nest there, but it's war for me down here.

DARZEE: For the great, the beautiful Rikki-tikki's sake I will stop. What is it, O Killer of the Terrible Nag?

RIKKI: Where does Nagaina keep her eggs?

DARZEE: In the melon bed. She hid them there weeks ago.

RIKKI: Fly off to the stables and pretend your wing is broken, and let Nagaina chase you away. I must get to the melon bed, and if I went there now she'd see me.

SNAKE CHARMER 2: Darzee was a feather-brained fellow, but his wife knew that cobra's eggs meant young cobras later on, so she flew off to trick Nagaina.

SNAKE CHARMER 1: When Deezar found Nagaina, she fluttered in front of the snake and cried out.

DEEZAR: Oh, my wing is broken! The boy in the house threw a stone at me and broke it.

SNAKE CHARMER 2: Then she fluttered more desperately than ever.

NAGAINA: *Hisss.* You warned Rikki-tikki when I would have struck him. You've chosen a bad time to be lame.

DEEZAR: The boy broke it with a stone!

NAGAINA: Before night, the boy will lie very still. *Hisss.* What is the use of running away? I am sure to catch you. Little fool, look at me!

SNAKE CHARMER 1: Darzee's wife knew better, for a bird who looks at a snake's eyes gets so frightened that she cannot move.

SNAKE CHARMER 2: Deezar fluttered along the ground, piping sorrowfully, and the snake quickened her pace.

SNAKE CHARMER 1: Once Rikki heard them going up the path, he raced to find Nagaina's eggs.

RIKKI: I am not a day too soon. The minute these hatch, they could each kill a man or a mongoose!

SNAKE CHARMER 2: A few minutes later, he heard Deezar screaming.

DEEZAR: Rikki-tikki, I led Nagaina down the path, and she has gone into the bungalow, and—oh, come quickly—she means to strike!

SNAKE CHARMER 1: Rikki took the last egg in his mouth and scuttled to the house.

> **Think About It**
>
> This play is a good example of *personification*. What do you think personification might mean?

Scene 5: The Bungalow and Garden

SNAKE CHARMER 1: Inside the bungalow, the family was just gathering for breakfast.

TEDDY: What are we having today, Mother? Something delightful, I hope.

ALICE: Isn't everything delightful in India? Especially after such a scare!

BIG MAN: Teddy, don't move!

ALICE: What is it?

BIG MAN: There's a cobra under Teddy's chair. Stay still, Teddy. Whatever you do, don't move!

NAGAINA: *Hisss.* Yes, stay still, son of the Big Man that killed Nag. If you move, I strike, and if you do not move, I strike. Oh, foolish people who killed my Nag!

SNAKE CHARMER 2: It was then that Rikki entered the room.

RIKKI: Turn around, Nagaina. Turn and fight!

NAGAINA: All in good time. I will settle my account with you shortly. *Hisss.* Look at your friends, Rikki-tikki. They are afraid. If you come a step nearer, I strike.

RIKKI: Look at your eggs in the melon bed. Go and look, Nagaina.

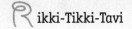

SNAKE CHARMER 1: The big snake turned half round and saw the one egg Rikki had brought with him.

NAGAINA: *Ah-h!* Give it to me.

RIKKI: What price for a snake's egg? For a young king cobra? For the last, the very last of the brood?

SNAKE CHARMER 2: Nagaina spun clear round, forgetting everything for the sake of the one egg.

SNAKE CHARMER 1: Teddy's father shot out a big hand, caught Teddy by the shoulder, and dragged him across the table, out of reach of Nagaina.

RIKKI: Tricked! Tricked! Tricked! *Rikk-tikk-tikk!* The boy is safe, and it was I—I who caught Nag by the hood last night in the bathroom.

SNAKE CHARMER 2: Then he began to jump, all four feet together, his head close to the floor.

RIKKI: It was over before the Big Man came. I did it. *Rikk-tikk-tikki!* Come, Nagaina, come and fight with me.

NAGAINA: Give me the egg! *Hisss.* Give me the last of my eggs, and I will go away.

RIKKI: Yes, you will go away, and you will never come back. Fight, widow! Fight!

CHORUS:
Eye to eye and head to head,
This shall end when one is dead;
Turn for turn and twist for twist—
Hah! The hooded Death has missed!

From whose *perspective* do we see this story? Would the story be different from Nagaina's perspective? How? What about the other characters?

SNAKE CHARMER 1: Rikki-tikki was staying just out of reach of Nagaina's bite, his little eyes like hot coals.

RIKKI: *Rikk-tikk-tikki!*

SNAKE CHARMER 2: Again and again she struck, each time coming within a whisker of Rikki.

RIKKI: *Rikk-tikk-tikki!*

SNAKE CHARMER 1: The egg still lay on the floor, till at last Nagaina snatched it in her mouth and flew like an arrow down the path with Rikki-tikki right behind her.

TEDDY: There, Father, the snake has gone into that hole! Rikki's little white teeth were clenched on her tail, and he went down with her!

BIG MAN: We can only hope he survives. Very few mongooses care to follow a cobra into its hole. In the dark, they never know when it might open out and give the cobra room to turn and strike.

ALICE: Oh, how very awful!

SNAKE CHARMER 2: The family watched and listened, but for a long time all was silent down the hole.

DARZEE: It is all over for Rikki-tikki! We must sing his death song, for Nagaina has surely killed him underground. Valiant Rikki-tikki is dead!

SNAKE CHARMER 2: Darzee cleared his throat and bowed his head when, suddenly, the grass by the hole quivered.

TEDDY: Here he is! Here is our Rikki at last!

ALICE: Why, hooray! Our mongoose has done it again!

RIKKI: It is all over. Nagaina will never come out again.

SNAKE CHARMER 1: This set everyone in the garden singing.

CHORUS: *Give him the Thanks of the birds,*
Bowing with tail-feathers spread!
Praise him with nightingale-words,
Nay, I will praise him instead.

SNAKE CHARMER 2: Rikki-tikki had a right to be proud of himself—but he did not grow too proud.

SNAKE CHARMER 1: And he kept that garden as a mongoose should keep it, with tooth and jump and spring and bit, till never a cobra dared show its head inside the walls.

CHORUS: *Who hath delivered us, who?*
Tell me his nest and his name.
Rikki, the valiant, the true,
Tikki, with eyeballs of flame!

> **Think About It**
>
> What is the theme of this story?

The Gift of the Magi

by O. Henry (United States, 1906)

This is a traditional retelling of the endearing story of a husband and wife who pawn their most precious things in order to buy gifts for each other, only to discover the gifts are no longer needed. The original story was written by William Sydney Porter, who wrote under the pen name O. Henry. He was famous for plot twists and surprise endings. Students will likely be familiar with the plot because it's been so readily adapted everywhere, from *Sesame Street* to *The Simpsons*, and even by Walt Disney.

Wise Man 1
Wise Man 2
Wise Man 3

Della: A young woman
Jim: Della's husband
Sydney: The janitor

Mrs. Porter: Della and Jim's neighbor
Madame Sophie: The wig maker
Shopkeeper

Vocabulary

possession, distinguished, cascade, ransacked, platinum, sophisticated, bargain, quibbling, precious, truant

Scene 1: New York City, Two Days Before Christmas, 1900

WISE MAN 1: We are the Magi.

WISE MAN 2: We invented the art of giving gifts at Christmas.

WISE MAN 3: Now, let us tell you of two people you might think are foolish . . .

WISE MAN 1: Two people who sacrificed the greatest treasures of their house . . .

WISE MAN 2: To celebrate Christmas.

WISE MAN 3: Their names were Della and Jim. They were a young married couple living in New York City.

DELLA: What a splendid walk that was!

JIM: Central Park at Christmas time is always delightful, Della.

DELLA: What shall we do now?

JIM: Let's walk down Broadway and window-shop.

DELLA: But we haven't any money.

JIM: It costs nothing to look. Besides, we can dream, can't we? Why, look here. Look at these scarves.

DELLA: Oh, wouldn't I be lovely wearing one of those?

JIM: Don't be silly. You're lovely just as you are.

DELLA: And look at those combs! I've admired them forever—pure tortoiseshell. Imagine how they'd look in my hair.

JIM: Della, your hair is already so long and beautiful. Look, it's almost to your knees.

DELLA: Do you think so, Jim? Do you really think it's beautiful?

JIM: I may be poor, Della, but I'm the luckiest man in New York!

How would you summarize what you know so far about the setting, the characters, their problems, and the plot?

Scene 2: Jim and Della's Apartment, the Next Morning

WISE MAN 1: Indeed, Jim was poor.

WISE MAN 2: He and Della lived in a shabby, one-room apartment.

WISE MAN 3: But Jim did have one possession of which he was proud: his pocket watch.

Why would Jim be proud of his watch? What does it say about his character?

JIM *(checking his watch)***:** I must be off to work, Della.

DELLA: Don't be long, Jim.

JIM: I'll put in my time and nothing more.

DELLA *(laughing)***:** You look so sophisticated when you glance at your watch.

JIM: Do I? Even with this old leather strap I use in place of a chain?

DELLA *(hugging him)***:** Who's to notice the strap when such a handsome man is holding such a glorious watch?

WISE MAN 1: Jim left for work. On the way out, he waved to the janitor, Sydney.

SYDNEY: Good morning, Mr. Young. Off to work already?

JIM *(checking his watch)***:** I can't afford to be late, Sydney.

SYDNEY: No, sir. That's quite a watch, sir.

JIM: It was my grandfather's. Keeps perfect time.

SYDNEY: It's quite remarkable, Mr. Young.

JIM: Sydney, about my mailbox.

SYDNEY: It says on it "Mr. James *Dillingham* Young," just like you asked.

JIM: That's just it. Perhaps it would be best if it just said "Mr. James *D.* Young."

SYDNEY: Oh, no, sir! *Dillingham* sounds so distinguished.

Why does Jim want his mailbox changed? What does that say about his circumstances?

JIM: Distinguished for a man who makes $30 a week—not for a man of a mere $20.

SYDNEY *(shaking his head)***:** Another pay cut, Mr. Young? Times are hard.

JIM *(again checking his watch)***:** Yes, they are, Sydney. But whether 20 or 30 a week, I must be on time.

Scene 3: Jim and Della's Apartment

WISE MAN 1: If Jim was poor, so too was Della.

WISE MAN 2: Her only treasure was her long, beautiful hair.

WISE MAN 3: Della and her neighbor sat together at the kitchen table.

DELLA *(counting coins)***:** Eighty-five, eighty-six . . . one dollar and eighty-seven cents. No matter how often I count it, Mrs. Porter, the amount never changes.

MRS. PORTER: Of course not, dear, but a penny saved is a penny earned.

DELLA: And how I've earned these pennies, Mrs. Porter. I've learned to drive a hard bargain: the grocer, the butcher, the milkman, I think they cringe when they see me coming—the worst cuts to save a penny, the bruised fruit to save two.

MRS. PORTER: Don't you worry now, honey. Things will turn around for you two. I just know it.

DELLA: But it's Christmas Eve. One dollar and eighty-seven cents! Whatever can I buy my wonderful Jim with one dollar and eighty-seven cents?

How would you describe Della? What are her positive traits? Does she have any negative traits?

MRS. PORTER: Now don't cry, Della.

WISE MAN 1: It was then that Della happened to glance in the mirror and caught sight of her long, beautiful hair, rippling and shining like a cascade of brown water.

WISE MAN 2: There she stood for a moment, a final tear splashing on the worn red carpet.

DELLA: I have it, Mrs. Porter.

WISE MAN 3: Her face grew pale as she quickly did her hair into a bun.

MRS. PORTER *(concerned)***:** Oh, Della, you mustn't!

DELLA: I must! For Jim. For Christmas.

WISE MAN 1: On went Della's old brown coat and old brown hat.

WISE MAN 2: And with a whirl of skirts and a brilliant sparkle still in her eye . . .

WISE MAN 3: She fluttered out the door and into the street.

Why do you think the author chose the word *fluttered* to describe Della's exit?

Scene 4: On Broadway

WISE MAN 1: Moments later, Della arrived at Madame Sophie's Hair Goods of All Kinds.

DELLA: Will you buy my hair?

MADAME SOPHIE: I buy hair. Take off your hat and let's have a look at it.

WISE MAN 2: Down rippled the brown cascade.

MADAME SOPHIE: What could be so important that you'd sacrifice such lovely hair?

DELLA: I'd sacrifice anything for my Jim. How much is it worth?

MADAME SOPHIE: Your hair? Twenty dollars.

DELLA: I'll take it. Give it to me quick.

WISE MAN 3: No longer was Della quibbling over pennies and bruised fruit.

DELLA: Now for Jim's present.

WISE MAN 1: For two hours, Della ransacked the stores, searching for that special something.

DELLA: He needs a new overcoat, and every day he goes off to work without gloves to warm his hands. But his gift must be something precious, something worthy of the honor of being owned by Jim.

WISE MAN 2: As soon as she saw it, she knew it was perfect.

SHOPKEEPER: May I help you?

DELLA: Might I see that watch chain?

SHOPKEEPER: Why, certainly, miss. It's platinum. A fine chain—but very expensive.

DELLA: It's so much like my husband. With a chain like this on his watch, he could check the time in anyone's company. How much is it?

SHOPKEEPER: Twenty-one dollars.

DELLA: I'll take it.

Think About It

What themes can you identify in this story?

At this time in history, $20 was a substantial amount of money, but let's do some math: How much money does Della have leftover?

Scene 5: The Apartment

WISE MAN 1: Back at the apartment, Della revealed to her friend what she'd done.

DELLA: How bad is it, Mrs. Porter?

MRS. PORTER: A pretty thing like you? You're adorable with or without your hair. We'll curl it. That's what we'll do. We'll curl it.

WISE MAN 2: Within 40 minutes, Della's head was covered with tiny curls.

MRS. PORTER: That's not so bad now, is it?

DELLA: If Jim doesn't faint before he takes a second look, he'll say I look like a truant schoolboy! A boy!

MRS. PORTER: Now, now.

DELLA: But what could I do?! What could I do with a dollar and eighty-seven cents?

MRS. PORTER: I'll go now, before Jim gets home.

DELLA: Yes, you had better. He's never late.

MRS. PORTER *(leaving)***:** Don't you worry now. It'll be all right.

DELLA *(aside)***:** Oh, please, let him think I'm still pretty!

WISE MAN 3: A moment after Mrs. Porter had left, in stepped Jim.

WISE MAN 1: As his eyes fixed on Della, he froze.

WISE MAN 2: He said nothing. He merely stood there with an odd expression on his face.

> **Think About It**
>
> Who is the story's main character, Jim or Della? Why do you think so?

DELLA: Jim, darling, don't stare at me that way. I had my hair cut off and sold because I couldn't have lived through Christmas without giving you a present! It'll grow back.

WISE MAN 3: But Jim seemed to be in a trance.

DELLA *(almost crying)***:** You don't mind, do you, Jim? My hair grows awfully fast. Jim? Say something, Jim. You can't imagine what a wonderful gift I have for you.

JIM *(confused)***:** You say you've cut off your hair?

DELLA *(crying)***:** Cut it off and sold it. Don't you like me just as well anyhow? I'm still me without my hair, aren't I?

WISE MAN 1: Jim looked around the room curiously.

JIM *(coming out of his trance)***:** You say your hair is gone?

DELLA: You needn't look for it. It's gone. I did it for you.

JIM *(hugging her)***:** Don't make any mistake, Della. I don't think there's anything in the way of a haircut or a shampoo that could make me love my girl any less. But if you unwrap this present, you'll see why you took me by surprise.

WISE MAN 2: Della unwrapped the gift and screamed for joy . . .

WISE MAN 3: Then cried aloud.

WISE MAN 1: For there lay the combs, the precious tortoiseshell combs she'd so long desired without hope of ever having.

DELLA *(sniffling)***:** My hair does grow fast, Jim.

WISE MAN 2: But Jim had not yet seen *his* present.

WISE MAN 3: She held it out to him in her open palm.

DELLA *(excited)***:** Isn't it dandy, Jim? You'll have to look at the time a hundred times a day now. Let's put it on your watch! I want to see how it looks!

WISE MAN 1: Jim tumbled onto the sofa and laughed.

JIM: Della, I sold the watch to get the money to buy your combs!

> Think About It
>
> What sequence of events leads to the story's conclusion?

DELLA: You didn't!

JIM: I did!

WISE MAN 2: Now, they laughed together.

JIM: Let's put our Christmas presents away and keep them for a while. They're too nice to use just yet. And now, suppose let's have some dinner. It's Christmas Eve!

WISE MAN 3: Today, we've told you of two foolish children . . .

WISE MAN 1: Who sacrificed their greatest treasures.

WISE MAN 2: But in a last word to the wise, let us conclude with this:

WISE MAN 3: Of all who give gifts, these two were the wisest.

WISE MAN 1: All those who sacrifice their earthly treasures to show love, they are wise.

WISE MEN *(together)***:** They are magi.

> Do you agree with the Magi's perspective? In what way have Jim and Della demonstrated wisdom or foolishness?

The Open Window

by Saki (H. H. Munro) (England, 1914)

H.H. Munro, who went by the pen name Saki, liked to write stories that resembled practical jokes. In "The Open Window," a man named Framton Nuttel comes to the countryside to recover from "a bad case of the nerves." Too bad he meets young Vera Sappleton, a teenaged trickster, who sends Framton over the edge. It's a great story for young readers because of its brevity, the way Munro sets up the victim, and because the lead character is a youngster. Be sure to let your students know the "window" is actually a set of French doors.

Cast of Characters

Narrator 1

Narrator 2

Vera: A teenaged trickster

Framton Nuttel: A nervous visitor from the city

Mrs. Sappleton: The lady of the house, Vera's aunt

Mr. Sappleton: Mrs. Sappleton's husband

Chuck: Mrs. Sappleton's son

Dave: Mrs. Sappleton's other son

Bertie: The spaniel

Vocabulary

stammered, tragedy, treacherous, faltered, snipe, scheming, pheasant, bog, eerily, coincidence

Scene: An Estate in the English Countryside, Early 1900s

NARRATOR 1: Teenaged girls come in many different packages.

NARRATOR 2: Some are shy. Some are silly.

NARRATOR 1: And some are smart and sassy.

NARRATOR 2: Young Vera was just that sort of girl—full of tricks and mischief.

VERA: My aunt will be down shortly. In the meantime, you must put up with me.

NARRATOR 1: Framton Nuttel, on the other hand, suffered from a bad case of the nerves.

FRAMTON NUTTEL *(nervously)***:** Umm. Very well. Umm.

NARRATOR 2: He very much wanted to say something to impress the girl, yet in his nervousness about meeting the aunt, he stammered and stuttered and managed to say just the wrong sort of thing.

FRAMTON NUTTEL *(stuttering)***:** It's my sister who insisted I introduce myself.

VERA: Your sister?

FRAMTON NUTTEL: Why, yes. When I told her I was going to the countryside, she said I would bury myself down here and not speak to a soul.

VERA: And yet, here you are.

FRAMTON NUTTEL: Yes, yes. Umm . . . it's good for the nerves, at least that's what my sister says. Meeting people is part of the *nerve cure* I'm supposed to be undergoing.

NARRATOR 1: This brought a long, awkward pause in the conversation.

NARRATOR 2 *(after some silence)***:** Mr. Nuttel fidgeted and blew his nose . . .

NARRATOR 1: While a scheming Vera made a quick study of him.

VERA: Do you know many of the people around here?

FRAMTON NUTTEL *(still stuttering)***:** Hardly a soul. My sister spent some time around here four years ago. She gave me letters introducing me to some of the local people.

How does Framton feel about his nerve cure, about meeting people?

NARRATOR 2: This he said in an unhappy tone.

VERA: So you don't know anything about my aunt?

FRAMTON NUTTEL: Only her name and address. My sister wrote it on this slip of paper here.

VERA: Then you know nothing about . . . about the *accident.*

FRAMTON NUTTEL: Accident?

VERA: Yes, her great tragedy happened just three years ago. That would be since your sister's time.

FRAMTON: In a restful country spot like this? Tragedies seem out of place.

NARRATOR 1: The girl pointed to a large set of French doors leading to the patio.

VERA: You may wonder why we keep that window wide open on an October afternoon.

This line says a lot about Framton's character. If you were Vera, how would you describe him to your teenaged friends later on?

NARRATOR 2: Mr. Nuttel nervously tugged at his starched collar and snugly fitting tie.

FRAMTON NUTTEL: It is rather warm for this time of year. But does that window have something to do with your aunt's tragedy?

VERA: It was out through that window three years ago to a day that my aunt's husband and her two young sons went off for their day's pheasant hunt. . . . They never came back.

NARRATOR 1: The girl whirled around and positioned herself so to direct Framton's attention out the window.

VERA: In crossing the field toward their favorite hunting ground, all three were swallowed up by a treacherous bog. It had been a most dreadfully wet summer. Places that were safe in other years gave way suddenly without warning. The most dreadful part, though, was that their bodies were *never* recovered.

NARRATOR 2: Here the girl's voice lost its matter-of-fact tone, and she dramatically faltered.

VERA: Poor Auntie always thinks they'll come back someday, they and the little brown cocker spaniel that was lost with them. Yes, she seems to think they'll walk through those doors, through that open window—just as they used to do!

FRAMTON NUTTEL: That . . . that is why she keeps the window open?

VERA: Poor, dear Auntie. She often told me how they went out, her husband with his white waterproof hunting coat over his arm, and Chuck, the oldest son, singing, "Bertie, why do you bound?" He always did that, sang, "Bertie, why do you bound?" to tease the spaniel. It got on the poor dog's nerves, he said.

NARRATOR 1: The girl turned eerily and stared out glossy-eyed through the open window.

Put it in your own words: How would you summarize what Vera has told Framton thus far?

VERA: You know, sometimes on still evenings like this, I almost get a creepy feeling that Auntie is right, that they will all come walking in through that window . . .

NARRATOR 2: She broke off with a shudder.

NARRATOR 1: It was a relief to Mr. Nuttel to see the aunt come hurrying in.

MRS. SAPPLETON: I'm so sorry to have kept you. I hope Vera has been amusing you?

FRAMTON NUTTEL *(still stuttering)***:** Umm. She has been very . . . she's been very . . . interesting.

NARRATOR 2: The aunt seated herself across from the guest. Meanwhile, in a flurry of skirts, Vera moved to stand directly behind her.

MRS. SAPPLETON: I hope you don't mind the open window. *My husband and our boys* will be home soon from shooting, and they always come in this way.

NARRATOR 1: Behind the aunt, the niece covered her heart with the palm of her hand and shook her head as if to say, *tsk, tsk.*

Vera is the story's *antagonist.* What do you think an antagonist is?

MRS. SAPPLETON: They've been out in the soggy fields hunting pheasant, so they'll make a fine mess all over my poor carpets. It's so like you menfolk to come stomping in, covered with mud from the bogs!

NARRATOR 2: Mrs. Sappleton rattled on cheerfully.

MRS. SAPPLETON: There have been very few birds lately. I don't think it will be much of a duck season at all.

NARRATOR 1: To Framton, it was all purely horrible. He tried to change the subject.

FRAMTON NUTTEL: The doctors tell me my illness comes from some kind of *disorder.*

NARRATOR 2: He became aware that Mrs. Sappleton was giving him only a tiny bit of her attention.

MRS. SAPPLETON: They tell me snipe is their best bet.

NARRATOR 1: And her eyes were constantly straying past him to the open window and the fields beyond.

NARRATOR 2: It was certainly an unfortunate coincidence, thought Mr. Nuttel, that he should visit on such a tragic anniversary!

FRAMTON NUTTEL: They've ordered complete rest. In my condition, I'm not to have any *excitement* at all.

MRS SAPPLETON: I see . . . I do hope they get a duck!

FRAMTON NUTTEL: On the matter of my diet, they are not so much in agreement.

MRS. SAPPLETON: Is that right? There's nothing like a good, crisp duck right from the oven!

FRAMTON NUTTEL: Yes, some say asparagus and greens will help, while others say . . .

NARRATOR 1: Mrs. Sappleton was on the verge of a yawn when suddenly her face brightened.

MRS. SAPPLETON: Here they are at last! Just in time for tea! And don't they look as if they're muddy up to their eyeballs!

NARRATOR 2: Framton shivered slightly and looked toward the girl—only to find her with dazed horror in her eyes, staring out the open window.

MRS. SAPPLETON: I'm so glad you'll have the chance to meet them! After all, they are the men of the family.

NARRATOR 1: Framton swung around in his seat and looked through the window.

NARRATOR 2: In the deepening twilight, three ghostlike figures were walking across the lawn.

NARRATOR 1: Each carried a gun, and each was wearing a white rain slick splattered in mud.

CHUCK *(offstage)***:** Bertie, why do you bound?

NARRATOR 2: Meanwhile, Framton was grabbing wildly for his cane and hat.

CHUCK: Bertie! I say, Bertie, why do you bound?

What's going on in this scene? Are Framton and Mrs. Sappleton listening to each other? Is Mrs. Sappleton aware of Framton's illness?

These few lines represent the story's climax or "high point." Why do you think so?

". . . why do you bound?" The author put this phrase in for some very specific reasons. What does it mean and how do you think it relates to the rest of the story?

NARRATOR 1: The hallway, the gravel drive, and the front gate were dimly noted stages in Framton's panicked retreat.

NARRATOR 2: And a bicyclist coming down the road had to drive into a hedge to avoid colliding with him.

MR. SAPPLETON: Here we are, everyone! We're fairly muddy, but most of it's dry.

DAVE: Who was that running off as we came up?

CHUCK: He made that fellow on his bicycle crash into the shrubs!

MRS. SAPPLETON: A most extraordinarily odd little man. His name was Nuttel.

MR. SAPPLETON: Nuttel, you say?

MRS. SAPPLETON: That's right. He could only talk about his illnesses, and then he dashed off without a word of apology. It was as if he'd seen a ghost!

NARRATOR 1: It was here that our teenaged villainess spoke up.

VERA: I suspect it was the spaniel.

DAVE: Little Bertie here? Who would be afraid of little Bertie?

VERA: He told me he had an unnatural fear of dogs. Apparently, he was once hunted into a cemetery by a pack of wild dogs and had to spend the night in a newly dug grave with the snarling beasts grinning and foaming just above him.

MR. SAPPLETON: My goodness! What a tragedy!

VERA: Enough to make anyone lose his nerve!

NARRATOR 2: Yes, imagination on short notice was the girl's specialty.

Why does Framton run from the house?

How do you think this incident will change Framton? What do you predict might happen to him?

What does this last line mean? What does it say about Vera?

Name: ______________________________ Date: ______________

Literary Elements/Story Discussion

1 **What is the title of the story?**

2 **Who is the author?**

3 **Setting:** When and where does the story happen?

4 **Main character:** Who is the story about?

5 **Conflict:** What is the main character's problem?

6 **Resolution:** How does the main character fix the problem?

7 **Theme:** What is the universal idea behind the story?

8 **Moral:** What lesson are we supposed to learn from the story?

9 **Realism:** Is the story realistic or unrealistic? What evidence is there?

10 **Plot:** Retell or summarize the main events of the story in just a few sentences.

Play Performance Scoring Guide

Student: ______________________ Date: ______________ Grade Level: ________

Play: ______________________ Part: ______________________

	Fluency	Delivery	Stage Presence	Comprehension
Exceeds expectations	✳ Reads without error ✳ Intonation and expression consistently appropriate to character	✳ Consistently appropriate volume ✳ Pacing as if speaking naturally	✳ Projects toward audience ✳ Memorizes lines ✳ Acts and puts character in voice, speaks with accent, etc. ✳ Recognizes cues without prompting ✳ Demonstrates leadership when practicing/performing ✳ May incorporate props where appropriate	✳ Able to identify and elaborate on literary elements and performance objections during discussion and assessment activities
Meets expectations	✳ Reads with minimal errors ✳ Some intonation and expressiveness	✳ Appropriately loud volume ✳ Consistent pacing	✳ Consistently faces audience ✳ Holds script away from face ✳ Attempts to act with voice characterization, etc. ✳ Follows along, recognizes cues ✳ Demonstrates cooperation when practicing	✳ Able to identify most literary elements and performance objectives during assessment activities ✳ Participates in discussions
Does not yet meet expectations	✳ Frequency or nature of errors suggests need for more practice ✳ Frequent stumbles, flat intonation, or lack of expression	✳ Too quiet ✳ Choppy or rushed pacing	✳ Tends to turn back to audience ✳ Tends to speak into script ✳ Does not add character—just reads lines ✳ Loses place, misses cues ✳ Tends to be unprepared or unfocused	✳ Does not participate in discussions ✳ Unable to identify most literary elements or performance objectives

Discussion Questions Answer Key

The Legend of Sleepy Hollow (page 7)

Page 8

The setting is in 1870, shortly after the American Revolution, in a small village called Sleepy Hollow.

Page 9 (top)

Brom is big and loud, probably a bully. He and Ichabod are alike only in that they're both young, unmarried, and interested in Katrina. Ichabod is a gentleman and might be described as "book smart." Brom might be called "street smart," athletic, and unscrupulous, creating something of a brains vs. brawn theme.

Page 9 (bottom)

The conflict centers around the pursuit of Katrina's hand in marriage. Ichabod's problem is that he is interested in Katrina despite Katrina's apparent relationship with Brom.

Page 10 (top)

Katrina's glance could mean that she's using Ichabod to make Brom jealous.

Page 10 (bottom)

Van Ripper, Van Ax, Vanderblood, etc. These characters are designed to create a ghostly mood.

Page 11 (top)

Possible themes include superstition, courtship, jealousy, brains vs. brawn.

Page 11 (bottom)

Ichabod probably asks for Katrina's hand in marriage, and she rejects him. Some believe she may have been unkind in her response, though there's no evidence presented within this play.

Page 12 (top)

These people are in Ichabod's thoughts and memory. He's recalling their words as he travels down the dark road.

Page 12 (bottom)

Answers will vary. "Head for the bridge" is one possible answer.

Page 13

Ichabod may have been carried off or scared away by the Horseman. He may have been killed or scared away by Brom pretending to be the Horseman.

The Nose (page 14)

Page 15

Ivan is disrespected. His wife calls him names, and the people in the street speak to him rudely.

Page 16

The Major's nose disappeared—presumably "cut off" by Ivan the Barber. It isn't possible, which is what makes the story a farce.

Page 17 (top)

Answers will vary.

Page 17 (bottom)

One theme could be that life is absurd, especially in Russian society of the 19th century. The author (Gogol) was criticizing the society in which he lived. Another theme is vanity. Kovalyov is vain or prideful. Losing his nose damages his image and standing in society.

Page 18

Of course the Nose knows nothing at all, he's just a nose! Yet here the Nose is talking. Notice also how the Nose accuses the Major of sniveling and how the Nose raises an eyebrow and glares!

Page 19

The Major is the main character. The story's problem (or conflict) is that he's lost his nose. The loss of the nose uncovers the Major's real problem: He is vain.

Page 20

The Inspector's statements are insulting to the Major because the Major is proud of his rank and his standing in society, yet the Inspector is suggesting he isn't respectable.

Page 21

Don't be vain. Don't put too much stock in appearances or rank. Physical attractiveness and social status are fleeting.

Page 22 (top)

The setting of this particular scene is an unknown street in the city in the days or weeks after the Major reacquired his nose. The people are spreading rumors about the Nose's activities.

Page 22 (bottom)

Perhaps the Major's concern speaks again to the story's absurdities, but some believe it shows how the Major is still focused on superficialities rather than substance. He didn't learn his lesson.

The Tell-Tale Heart (page 23)

Page 24 (top)

The story's setting might have made it scarier to the original readers because they might have seen it as something that could happen to them, as "true crime" instead of fiction.

Page 24 (middle)

Though the Raven Chorus says the narrator has lost his mind, the Narrator himself claims he is normal. Who should you believe? The crazy letter formatting helps convey the author's intent.

Page 24 (bottom)

Keen means sharp, focused, intense.

Page 25

Perhaps the eye bothers the narrator because he feels he is being watched and scrutinized. Perhaps the eye signifies humanity's judgment into his character or condition.

Page 26

The obvious answer is that the eye was open on the eighth night. But it is open only because the Narrator has frightened the Old Man.

Page 27 (top)

The Narrator wants the officers to see that he hasn't taken any of the Old Man's belongings, and therefore the Old Man must be safe. But it could also reveal that the narrator's crime was not about material possessions.

Page 27 (bottom)

To the Villainous Narrator it seems like the policemen have been there a long time, but he is merely feeling anxious because of his crime.

Page 28 (top)

The story is realistic. People really do go insane. After such a crime, the perpetrator's sense of guilt could make him believe he was hearing the beating heart.

Page 28 (bottom)

It is unrealistic to think the officers would remain so calm when such a terrible crime has been committed, which suggests they are unaware. The Narrator believes they are mocking him because of some of their comments about the countryside and people acting strangely.

Page 29

Some interpret the story to be the Narrator's confession at the police station or in a courtroom. But could one also believe the Narrator next attacks the three officers and is now confessing only the original crime to the audience? The final line, which doesn't occur in Poe's original, suggests the Narrator may now attack the audience merely because they are staring at him in the same way the Old Man had (and perhaps the same way the officers must have).

A Christmas Carol (page 30)

Page 31

Ghost and *dead* appear twice within the first two lines, establishing a dark mood.

Page 32 (top)

Scrooge's only goal seems to be that of accumulating money. Although apparently quite rich, she lives like a miser. Elizabeth, while apparently not rich, has a healthy, balanced life view. She is focused on relationships—even with nasty old Scrooge!

Page 32 (bottom)

The line shows how Scrooge, being miserly, has made her house so dark and scary that the appearance of ghosts makes sense. Would the story seem as plausible if Scrooge lived in a warm, bright, and cheerful place?

Page 33

Marley says each link in the chain represents a kind deed left undone, therefore the chain represents all the nastiness or sins of its owner. Scrooge's chain is apparently much longer and heavier than Marley's.

Page 34 (top)

The ghost is using something like reverse psychology to get Scrooge to admit she once enjoyed Christmas, which apparently she did before becoming consumed by money.

Page 34 (bottom)

Answers will vary. Isn't it considered prudent today for young women to complete their education and establish their careers before marrying? Had Scrooge married, would she have ultimately sacrificed the marriage in pursuit of wealth? Or would she have led a life more like that of Mrs. Cratchit?

Page 35 (top)

The ghost is reminiscent of Santa Claus.

Page 35 (bottom)

The fact that Scrooge cares what happens to Tiny Tina shows there is still some good in her.

Page 36

It could be realistic because Scrooge falls asleep and wakes in her own house, so it is possible she dreamt all the ghostly events. Note that everything that happens to everyone else is entirely realistic. Only Scrooge "sees" the ghosts.

Page 37

Scrooge has learned to value people and human relationships instead of just money. She has become compassionate. Whether she changed because she felt compassion for the Cratchits or because she feared dying alone is open to interpretation.

The Necklace (page 38)

Page 39

The problem is that Matilda is discontent.

Page 40 (top)

Mad means crazy here.

Page 40 (bottom)

The main character in a story is usually the one with the problem. Therefore, students could argue that Loisel is the main character. His problem is that he has a discontented wife. However, the main character of a story is also the one who changes. Matilda is the main character, because at the end of the story, she is the one who has most profoundly changed.

Page 41

Maupassant is speaking to Madame Forestier, but, of course, all she hears is the cat meowing or purring.

Page 42 (top)

Because Matilda is so focused on appearances, she would have a difficult time choosing from among all the jewels.

Page 42 (bottom)

Because a cat and mouse serve as the narrators, the story appears unrealistic (after all, cats cannot talk), but Matilda's story itself is realistic.

Page 44 (top)

Loisel retraces their steps and goes to the cab company and the police station. They lie to Forestier to buy some time, and then they borrow money to purchase a replacement. They then spend ten years working to pay off the debt.

Page 44 (bottom)

Matilda has grown older, but more importantly, because she has had to work so hard, she no longer appears respectable. In her quest to appear wealthy for the ball, she has, in the long run, become bedraggled and poor-looking.

Page 45 (top)

Matilda goes from being well-off and discontent to being poor and "decently content." Contentment came through being free of debt rather than through accumulating wealth.

Page 45 (bottom)

Possible answers: Don't take for granted what you have. Be content. Be honest. Don't focus on appearances.

Rikki-Tikki-Tavi (page 46)

Page 47

This story takes place during the era of England's occupation of India (1800s) in the bungalow of English citizens working there.

Page 48 (top)

Cobras are too dangerous for the garden; Rikki must protect the garden's residents.

Page 48 (bottom)

Answers will vary. Some students may talk about "the natural order" and "the circle of life." Others may talk about birds already being "alive." Some creative thinker might answer, "Rikk-tikk-tikki."

Page 49

Rikki is presented as brave or valiant, while Chuchundra is weak and frightened. Chuchundra's character is meant to show that the garden creatures live in constant fear of the cobras.

Page 50 (top)

The water jar shows that this story happened in the distant past, before people had houses with full plumbing.

Page 50 (bottom)
Snake eggs hatch into snakes, which will be just as dangerous as their parents.

Page 51
The story is unrealistic because the animals talk to one another, although from the perspective of the Big Man and his family, who conceivably hear only chattering from the creatures, it could be construed as realistic.

Page 52
Personification means non-humans demonstrating human emotions and traits. The animals talking and thinking like humans is a form of personification.

Page 53
Most of the story is from Rikki's perspective (although the family's perspective is also seen, such as in scenes 1 and 5). The story is much different from the perspective of the cobras.

Page 54
One theme is courage. Rikki fights the cobras and defends the garden. His courage leads to him becoming a hero.

The Gift of the Magi (page 55)

Page 56
The story focuses on a young couple living in New York City around the turn of the 20th century. The "window shopping" shows they're so poor they can't afford to buy Christmas presents.

Page 57 (top)
The watch makes Jim feel important and distinguished. It may show that he aspires to become a success. It shows that he's conscious of time—one has only a limited amount of time in life to accomplish one's goals. Perhaps it also shows that he is somewhat superficial.

Page 57 (bottom)
Jim's pay cut has been a blow to his self-esteem. He does not feel distinguished.

Page 58 (top)
Della is apparently pretty, she is a loving wife, and she works hard at being frugal. She may be a bit childish.

Page 58 (bottom)
The author wants you to see Della's innocence, like that of a little bird.

Page 59 (top)
Likely themes include love, generosity, poverty, wisdom vs. folly.

Page 59 (bottom)
Della has eighty-seven cents, which wasn't much.

Page 60
Both Jim and Della seem to have equal standing. Both characters change by making sacrifices and then seeing that their sacrifices were unnecessary.

Page 61 (top)
It's Christmas Eve, and Jim and Della wish to show their love for each other by purchasing gifts. Because they're poor, Jim sells his watch to buy Della a gift for her hair. Meanwhile, Della sells her hair to buy Jim a gift for his watch. When they share their gifts, they realize the purchases were unnecessary.

Page 61 (bottom)
Answers will vary. Students may say that Jim and Della were wise in that they were willing to part with their material things to show love for each other. Others may say they were foolish to sell what was precious to them just to buy material things. They could express their love without wasting their money. Would they have been wiser to sell their items and put the money in savings?

The Open Window (page 62)

Page 64 (top)
The fact that Framton speaks in an "unhappy tone" suggests he doesn't like it. The original story says he replies "in a tone of distinct regret."

Page 64 (bottom)
Answers will vary: Vera might describe Framton as geeky, nervous, strange, freaky, etc. The fact that Framton is wearing a starched shirt and tie suggests he wishes to impress; the fact that he tugs on his tie shows how uncomfortable he is.

Page 65 (top)
Vera has told Framton that her uncle, cousins, and the family dog went hunting three years earlier but drowned in a bog. She's implied the aunt is a bit crazy, that she can't accept the fact that her family is dead, and that she leaves the French doors open because she thinks they'll all return from hunting any minute.

Page 65 (bottom)
An antagonist is a character that antagonizes, or causes the conflict in a story.

Page 66 (top)
Although Framton and Mrs. Sappleton are both talking about food, they are not listening to each other. Although Framton has mentioned his illness, Mrs. Sappleton is giving him "only a tiny bit of her attention." Framton focuses on his illness and Vera's interjections, while the aunt focuses on the returning hunters. (Ironically, they are equally nervous.) This all works to Vera's advantage.

Page 66 (middle)
It's at this point that Mrs. Sappleton sees her family returning (which eases her own nerves); here that Framton believes he's seeing ghosts (which overstimulates his nervousness); and here that Vera's prank pays off.

Page 66 (bottom)
The hunter is asking the spaniel why she jumps around so much. It's a rhetorical question; the best answer is "just because." Why does Vera play this prank on Framton? Just because. The question also prompts the reader to consider why Framton bounds from the house.

Page 67 (top)
Framton believes he's seeing the ghosts of the hunters. Because of his nervous disorder and the sincerity of Vera's story, he's unable to think rationally at this point.

Page 67 (middle)
Answers will vary. Framton's encounter with Vera has worsened his condition. He'll likely forgo his nerve cure and head back to the city for more sessions with his doctor, stuttering and tugging on his collar more than ever.

Page 67 (bottom)
Vera has a quick wit (or she's a good liar), which allows her to take advantage of people and circumstances.